A SCOTLAND YARD MURDER CASEBOOK

The Story of Nine Murders and One Detective

Simon Lewis

Contents

Introduction

During Percy Savage's long career as a detective he was involved in some of Scotland Yard's most notorious murder cases.

Some of these cases were notable for being gruesome. For example, the 'Camberwell Triple Murder' involved victims whose bodies were mutilated, dismembered and beheaded before being transported across London in a furniture van, and buried in a suburban back garden. In the 'Eastbourne Love Experiment Murder' the body of the victim — the pregnant lover of the murderer — was cut up and stored in a trunk, a biscuit tin and a hat box: parts of the body were then disposed of by being thrown out of a moving train.

Other cases dealt with by Savage became well known simply because they remain mysteries. The 'Luard Case' — in which the wife of a retired Major-General was shot in woodland in Kent — remains unsolved to this day, despite extensive speculation about the identity of the murderer. Similarly, the 'Camberley Mystery' (involving a double throat-slitting and hammer attack) remains unsolved.

Other cases which Savage investigated were fascinating because of the high emotional drama involved. The 'Tragedy of Two Army Doctors' involved a murder by an officer who had been decorated for gallantry on the Western Front. He returned home after the First World War to find that his marriage was in tatters, and that his wife wanted a divorce. He then shot another officer, blaming him for the disintegration of his marriage.

'A Scotland Yard Murder Casebook' brings together a selection of murder cases in which Percy Savage was involved.

Savage became a Detective Constable in 1901, and retired as a Detective Superintendent in 1934. 'A Scotland Yard Murder

Casebook' gives a clear insight into how policing, and murder investigation, changed during this period.

According to Percy Savage:

"When I joined there was not a single telephone at Scotland Yard or at any of the stations. A telegraph was installed in the principal stations, but if the public wanted the police they had to fetch them. There were no motor cars. A horse and trap was provided for the Superintendent to tour his Division. If a police officer was engaged on an urgent inquiry, he was permitted to take a horse-drawn omnibus or tramcar; otherwise he walked to save expense. A horsed dispatch van took a whole day to convey important papers from Scotland Yard to the outside stations. Finger prints were unknown, and old criminals were identified by unreliable photographs or personal recognition. Policemen carried heavy oil lamps on their belts. Oil lamps and even candles were the illumination at many police stations. There were no women police . . . "

However, by the time that Percy Savage retired as a Detective Superintendent in 1934, the world of Scotland Yard had changed beyond recognition. Telephones, radios, cars and finger printing were all firmly entrenched in police work. In 1934, for the first time, the public were able to use a special phone number (Whitehall 1212) to contact Scotland Yard; it was also in this year that women were first allowed to become detectives.

It was not just Scotland Yard which changed during the course of Savage's career — according to Savage, criminals changed as well. Writing in the 1930s, Savage claimed that:

"the criminals of twenty and thirty years ago were cleverer, more daring and more enterprising than the criminals of today. The introduction of the motor car has made life easy and less risky for criminals. The motor car gave him considerably increasing facilities both for committing a crime and escaping detection."

After retiring in 1934, Savage wrote his memoirs — 'Savage of Scotland Yard' — and it is from these memoirs that the murder cases in 'A Scotland Yard Murder Casebook' are drawn.

A 'Scotland Yard Murder Casebook' should appeal to anybody interested in classic or vintage true murder stories.

HOW TO DISPOSE OF A CORPSE

* * *

One problem a murderer sometimes faces is how to dispose of a body (or bodies).

'Secrets of the Locked Bag' concerns a case which the renowned pathologist, Sir Bernard Spilsbury, described as the most gruesome on which he had ever worked.

'The Camberwell Triple Murder' deals with the murder of a whole family, followed by an attempted murder.

* * *

1 Secrets of the Locked Bag

"He had already partly dismembered the body, and he now set to work with the intention of disposing of the remains. The day was dark and heavy. He built a huge fire in the room, and on this placed the head. At that moment the storm broke with an appalling crash of thunder and a violent flash of lightning. As the head lay upon the coals, the dead eyes opened, and Mahon, in his shirtsleeves, fled blindly out to the rain-swept shingle of the deserted shore. When he nerved himself to return the fire had done its work."

Edgar Wallace, 'The Trial of Patrick Mahon'

* * *

Waterloo Station, London
The Crumbles, Eastbourne
1924

* * *

Patrick Mahon had the perfect job for a man who wished to get up to things without his wife knowing. Mahon was a sales manager for the Consols Automatic Aerators company in Sunbury-on-Thames. The company made soda fountains, and Mahon was required to spend long periods away from home selling its products, often staying in hotels. Ironically, it was his wife, Jessie, who had helped him to get a job at the firm in the first place. She was employed at Consols Automatic Aerators as a cashier and secretary, and had put a good word in for him when a suitable vacancy came up.

At the end of April 1924, Jessie Mahon was a worried woman. Her husband had spent the last two weekends away from the couple's home in Pagoda Avenue, Richmond. Patrick Mahon had

had an affair earlier in their marriage: was he having another affair now? Jessie Mahon also found out that her husband had secretly spent a whole day at Plumpton race course — by chance, a mutual acquaintance had spotted Mahon there, and had duly reported the fact to his wife. Patrick Mahon enjoyed a flutter on the horses, and his wife was concerned that he may be spending too much on gambling at the races.

Her curiosity aroused, Jessie Mahon decided to search her husband's clothes. The search revealed a cloakroom ticket for a bag which had been deposited at Waterloo station. This made her even more suspicious: why would her husband need to keep a bag at a London railway station? She consulted a friend called John Beard, a former Divisional Detective Inspector in the Metropolitan Police, and Beard agreed to go to Waterloo station with her, to investigate further.

At Waterloo, Beard gave in the cloakroom ticket, and was handed a Gladstone bag — a wide, sturdy bag — in return. The bag was locked, but by pulling open the sides Beard could peer inside, where he saw a large knife and some silk covered in bloodstains. Beard was now in a quandry: what should he tell Jessie Mahon? He decided that it was best, at this stage, not to tell her about the disturbing discovery. Instead, he returned the bag to the cloakroom, and reassured Jessie Mahon that there was nothing to do with horse-racing or betting in it. He also told her to put the cloakroom ticket back where she had found it, in the pocket of one of her husband's suits.

Then, Beard contacted Scotland Yard.

* * *

In 1924, Percy Savage had just been promoted to Detective Chief Inspector. He accepted the promotion with some regrets, because it meant moving away from the day-to-day life of a Division. It did, however, bring him into direct involvement with the Mahon case. He was one of the first officers to be told about the strange discovery of a bag containing a knife and bloodstained silk at Waterloo station.

Savage went to the station to look at the bag. He extracted a small portion of the bloodstained silk, and then returned the bag to the cloakroom. Back at Scotland Yard, Savage sought scientific advice about the blood on the silk, and was told that it was likely to be human.

Savage ordered Detective Sergeant Frew and Detective Sergeant Thompson to stay at Waterloo station and keep watch on the cloakroom. Their instructions were simple: anybody who turned up at the left luggage office with the cloakroom ticket for the bag was to be detained.

Luck was on their side. At 6.15 p.m. the next day, Friday 2 May, Patrick Mahon walked up to the cloakroom, and handed in his cloakroom ticket. As Mahon took the bag from the attendant, Frew and Thompson drew up on either side.

"We are police officers. Is that your bag?"

Mahon smiled, and replied "I believe it is".

When Mahon was told that he must accompany the officers to Kennington Road police station, he replied "Rubbish".

Detective Chief Inspector Savage was telephoned from Kennington Road police station, to tell him that Patrick Mahon had been detained. Together with Detective Inspector Hall, he went immediately to Kennington Road. Savage later recalled the moment he first set eyes on Mahon:

"Mahon stood up and received me with a pleasant smile. He was a man above the average height, and was dressed in a well-made dark brown lounge suit, a brown tie, and brown shoes. His brown soft hat, tanned gloves, and folded umbrella lay on the table. A man of athletic build, well groomed. His brown curly hair, tinged with grey, was neatly brushed over an intellectual forehead. He had a well-formed mouth, and a healthy clean-shaven face."

Savage decided to take Mahon to Scotland Yard by taxi. Throughout the journey, Mahon remained silent, keeping up an air of indifference. At Scotland Yard, Savage took him to a private room where, using a key which had been found in Mahon's pocket, he opened the bag which had been deposited at Waterloo. Savage placed the items in the bag carefully on the table in front of Mahon, bringing them out one by one.

Eventually, on the table in front of Mahon, lay some torn silk women's underwear, two pieces of white silk, a blue silk scarf, a large kitchen knife, some disinfectant powder, and a canvas tennis racket bag bearing the initials "E.B.K.". All of the silk items were stained with grease and blood.

Savage asked Mahon to explain how he came to be in possession of these things.

Mahon now had to think fast. How much did the police know? Possessing blood stained silk underwear — or any of the other items in the bag — was not a criminal offence. The contents of the bag did not, on their own, prove that Mahon had committed any crime. Mahon could simply play his cards close to his chest, and leave the police guessing, if he chose. The police would be forced to release him without charge.

Mahon was under pressure, however, and felt that he had to give some kind of explanation. He told Detective Inspector Savage that he used the bag to carry home meat for dogs.

Savage knew immediately that Mahon was lying. Nobody would use silk to wrap pet food, or go to the trouble of leaving a bag of this sort in the cloakroom of a railway station.

It was then that Savage played his ace card: "But this is human blood."

Mahon was clearly unnerved. At first, Mahon stayed silent, but then tried to insist again that the bag was used for carrying dog's meat. Savage and Mahon looked intently at each other across the table.

Then Mahon made a terrible error. "You seem to know all about it", he said to Savage.

Of course, Savage knew nothing about it; in fact, he didn't even know what 'it' was. Scotland Yard did not have a body, or a crime scene, or even a report of a missing person.

Then Mahon repeated "You seem to know all about it."

Now, Savage had to bluff. "It's not for me to tell you what I know," he told him. "It's for you to tell me what you know."

Mahon was unsure what to do next. He leant forward, resting his chin on his right hand. Glancing at Savage from time to time, he stayed in this pose for at least a quarter of an hour, before sitting up. Then he spoke slowly but cryptically: "I wonder if you can realize how terrible a thing it is for one's body to be active, and one's mind to fail to act."

It was now approaching 11 p.m., but Savage decided to play a long game. He offered Mahon refreshments and told him that he was in no hurry, and that he should take his time. Mahon sat silently for another three quarters of an hour, only breaking his silence to explain to Savage that he was considering his position.

In the background, Savage could hear the ticking of the clock hanging on the wall. He knew that silence — the unbearable tension of silence — was the only weapon he had. Then, as midnight approached, Mahon started to crack. Standing up, he said "I suppose you know everything. I will tell you the truth."

After being cautioned that he had the right to remain silent, but that anything that he did say would be taken down and might be used in evidence against him, Mahon started dictating a statement, which was written down by Inspector Hall.

What followed was, according to Savage, "the most amazing statement I have ever heard in my long career". The length of the statement can be seen from the fact that it took Mahon two and a half hours to complete it. Savage described Mahon's demeanour during that two and a half hours:

"He spoke with emphasis and studied deliberation. He weighed each word carefully, made corrections whenever he thought he had not made his meaning quite clear, and after each sentence he paused and formed the next sentence in his own mind before giving utterance to it. During the whole of this time he was perfectly self-possessed and calm, and a stranger entering the room might have imagined he was the head of a firm dictating a very delicate and important business letter."

Mahon started by explaining that he had met "the woman" about ten months earlier, although he did not give "the woman" a name. He may have thought that Savage already knew the identity of the "the woman"; alternatively, perhaps he was trying to test exactly how much Savage knew.

Mahon said that he and "the woman" had gone to a bungalow outside Eastbourne on Saturday 12 April. On Wednesday 16 April, they had gone to London for the day, returning to the bungalow that evening. At the bungalow, the couple had quarrelled:

"In a violent temper she threw an axe at me. It was a coal axe. It hit me a glancing blow. Then I saw red. We fought and struggled. She was a very big strong girl. She appeared to be quite mad with anger and rage. During our struggle we overturned a chair, and her head fell on an iron coal scuttle, and it appeared (not more or less) to stun her. This happened about twelve o'clock, midnight. I attempted to revive her, but found I could not.

The reaction after the struggle having set in, the consequences to me came home with stunning force. I put the body in the spare bedroom and covered it up with her fur coat. I came up to London on the morning of April 17th and returned to the bungalow fairly late, taking with me a knife which I had bought in a shop in Victoria Street. I also bought at the same shop a small saw.

When I got back to the bungalow I was still so upset and worried that I could not then carry out my intentions to decapitate the body. I did so on Good Friday [18th April]. I severed the legs from the hips, the head, and left the arms on. I then put the various parts in a trunk in the bedroom and locked the door.

On Saturday, April 19th, I stayed at the bungalow, also Sunday the 20th, and came back to London on Monday, the 21st. I did not touch the body either on Saturday, Sunday, or Monday. I again went to the bungalow on Tuesday, the 22nd, and on that day I burned the head in the sitting-room grate, and also the feet and legs.

I came back to town late on Tuesday night or Wednesday morning. I went down again on Friday night, April 25th, and stayed at an hotel that night, going over to the bungalow about ten o'clock on Saturday morning. I had to cut up the trunk. I also cut off the arms. I burned portions of them. The smell was appalling and I had to think of some method of disposing of the portions.

I then boiled some portions in a large pot in the bungalow, cut the portions up small, packed them in the brown bag, and I threw them out of the train while travelling between Waterloo and Richmond. These portions were not wrapped up in anything. This was about ten o'clock on Sunday night. The bag to which I refer is the one now produced to me.

I had intended to go home on Sunday night, but as I could not dispose of the portions between Waterloo and Richmond, I went on to Reading and stayed at the Station Hotel in the name of Rees. Next morning I came to London and left the bag in the cloakroom at Waterloo station.

I had disposed of the remaining pieces between Waterloo and Reading on April 27th. The bloodstained cloth that was in the bag was a pair of bloomers that I got out of the girl's trunk. I tore them up and used it to wrap up some of the flesh."

Having given his account of the struggle, the accidental death of the "woman" and the difficulties in disposing of the body, Mahon finally filled in a key detail:

"The woman's name is Emily Beilby Kaye, a single woman, aged 29, an educated person, and when I first knew her ten months ago was secretary to the receiver of the company where I was employed."

In fact, Emily Kaye was 37 years old (it appears that she had told Mahon that she was 29). It was true, however that Emily Kaye was single and well-educated (in the various jobs in which she worked, she acquired a reputation for competence and effectiveness). When Mahon first met Emily Kaye she was working for a firm of Chartered Accountants which had been appointed to act as receivers of Mahon's employers, Consols Aerators, after Consols got into financial difficulty.

Mahon then went back over other aspects of his statement. He added that the quarrel on the night of Emily Kaye's death had started on the train down from London, and continued at the bungalow between 9 and 10 p.m., not midnight as he had said before:

"At the time of the quarrel in the bungalow she had removed her fur coat and hat, and was wearing a greenish-grey heather costume. All the clothing Miss Kaye was wearing is now at the bungalow, including stockings and shoes. The two pieces of white silk were in Miss Kaye's trunk and were used by me in wrapping up portions of the flesh. The powder in the bag is a disinfectant which I used because of the ghastly smell.

It was about 6.15 today (May 2nd) when I went to Waterloo and got my bag from the cloakroom, intending to go to Victoria and take it with me to the bungalow, as there are still some portions of the body remaining in the trunk.

The cause of the quarrel occurred in this way. I had arranged with Miss Kaye to do certain things, but my better nature prevailed. This appeared to inflame her with the result that she threw a missile, which, although hitting me, did not injure me beyond a bruise. The rest followed as I have already said."

Mahon finished dictating and signing his statement by about 3 a.m.. Savage thought that Mahon looked "very pleased with himself" as he checked through his statement: it was as if Mahon was convinced that he had given a plausible explanation of how Emily Kaye had met an accidental death, and why he had disposed of her body. Mahon was now extremely tired, and asked Savage if he could have a spot of whisky, a request to which Savage readily agreed.

* * *

Detective Chief Inspector Savage knew that it was now important to get down to Eastbourne without delay. Borrowing a Flying Squad van, he left Scotland Yard with Inspector Hall, Inspector McBride and a photographer.

In the early morning of 3 May, the Scotland Yard team arrived at the Crumbles, a long stretch of shingle, running between Eastbourne and Pevensey Bay. This was the location of the bungalow identified by Mahon. The team also met Superintendent Sinclair, from the East Sussex police, who had come from nearby Hailsham.

The Crumbles already had a certain notoriety. In 1920, the dead body of Irene Munro, a seventeen year old typist who had been on holiday at Eastbourne had been found here. She had been bludgeoned to death with a brick. Now, four years later, Scotland Yard returned to the same shingle beach.

The bungalow which Mahon had described in his statement was known as the "Officer's House". It was detached, forming part of a range of old Coastguard cottages, close to the Eastbourne road. From the cottages, the beach sloped down to the sea.

The approach to the bungalow, through a gate and up a flagstone path to a porch surrounded by climbing roses, was attractive. However, what struck officers as they opened the front door of the bungalow was the smell — a disgusting stench which hinted at what might be found inside.

The front door of the bungalow opened directly on to the sitting room, which had a simple domestic cosiness about it. The sitting room wallpaper was printed with a design of shrubs in plant pots, and there was an open fire place, a carpet, a sofa, a chair, a cupboard and two oil lamps. Beyond the sitting room was a passageway, a dining room, four bedrooms, a kitchen and a bathroom converted from a scullery.

The source of the smell soon became obvious. In a fireplace there was a large saucepan full of a reddish fluid topped with a thick layer of grease: under the grease were pieces of boiled human flesh still with skin attached. The fender in front of the fire had grease splashes on it and, nearby, there was a saucer full of solidified fat. In the scullery-bathroom, a galvanized iron bath and saucepan contained boiled human remains. In the grate of the sitting-room fire place there were fragments of burned bone. More fragments of burned bone were found in the dining room fire place.

In one of the bedrooms, on the right of the passage which ran through the bungalow, there was a rusty saw which had grease and a piece of flesh stuck to it. There was also a hat box, a large trunk painted with the initials "E.B.K.", and a leather kit-bag containing a brush, a comb, jewellery and a gold wrist-watch.

The trunk contained four large pieces of human body, unboiled. In a hat box, together with stained items of women's clothing, there were 37 separate pieces of flesh, which had been boiled: the pieces had either been sawn or cut. There was also a biscuit tin, containing a human heart and internal organs.

A search of the bungalow revealed an axe with a broken handle, a number of articles of women's clothing which were greasy and bloodstained, and a cauldron-shaped metal coal-scuttle supported on three metal legs. One of the coal-scuttle's legs was bent and had specks of blood on it.

The carpet in the bungalow was heavily bloodstained. In some places, blood had soaked through to the felt underlay and the floor boards. The pattern of bloodstains suggested that Emily Kaye had died or collapsed in the sitting room, before being dragged through the passageway to a bedroom, and then into the bathroom. The butchery of the body appeared to have taken place in the bathroom.

Detective Chief Inspector Savage placed a police guard on the bungalow with strict instructions — nobody was to be admitted, and the contents of the bungalow were not to be touched. He then telephoned Lieutenant Colonel Ormerod, the Chief Constable of East Sussex. As the murder had taken place in East Sussex, in principle it was now the responsibility of the local force, and nothing to do with Scotland Yard. However, Ormerod made the decision straight away that Scotland Yard should continue to run the investigation.

With the bungalow locked up and guarded, Percy Savage returned to London, arriving at Scotland Yard at midnight. He had hardly had any sleep since the day before, but sleep had to wait when he was told that Mahon had made a new statement.

In this statement, Mahon said that the fatal quarrel in the bungalow had taken place on Thursday 15 April (and not Good Friday, 16 April, as he had originally stated). He also added a surprising new element to the story. On 16 April, when Emily Kaye's body was lying in the Crumbles bungalow, Mahon said that he had returned to London and met a woman called Ethel Duncan. Mahon and Duncan had gone to Eastbourne the following day, and stayed in the bungalow.

Mahon's new statement also gave further information about his relationship with Emily Kaye, in particular about what became known as the 'love experiment'.

According to Mahon, soon after he met Kaye in 1923, she told him that she was particularly fond of him. Kaye was aware that Mahon was married: she knew his wife by sight and had spoken to her on the telephone. Towards the end of the summer of 1923, she invited Mahon on a river trip. A physical relationship followed. As Mahon put it:

"As a result, I realized that she was a woman of the world, which . . . came rather as a surprise to me."

Just before Christmas 1923, Emily Kaye was made redundant. With time on her hands, she put pressure on Mahon to see more of her. Mahon resisted this, but Kaye was insistent:

"She told me quite plainly that she wished my affection and was determined to win it if possible . . . From that moment I felt more or less at the mercy of a strong-minded woman whom, although I liked her in many ways, I did not tremendously care for. She became thoroughly unsettled, and begged me to give up everything and go abroad with her. She informed me of her great love and affection for me, but I plainly told her I could not agree to such a course. I agreed to consider the matter in the hope of gaining time."

Kaye told Mahon that she wanted him to give up his job, and go with her to Paris for a while, before emigrating to South Africa where the couple could start a new life.

When Kaye realised that Mahon was hesitant about this plan, she proposed a 'love experiment'. The experiment would involve the couple living together for a short while, in order to convince Mahon that Kaye was the woman for him:

"She suggested that I should take a holiday and go away with her for a week or two and take a bungalow where we would be alone together, and where she would convince me with her love that I could be perfectly happy with her. I again refused, but she insisted and told me that she had determined to gain and retain my affection somehow . . .

Ultimately I agreed. I arranged to take the bungalow at Eastbourne for two months, and Miss Kaye suggested that I take it in an assumed name and haphazardly fixed on the name Waller . . . She felt convinced that the spot and the nature of the bungalow would be ideal . . . She admired the whole place, particularly the garden. She was charmed with the place . . . "

Mahon's new statement also gave a further account of the quarrel on the day of Kaye's death. As Mahon admitted, he had strung Kaye along, in an attempt to buy time. As part of this deception, Mahon told Kaye that he would apply for a passport. However, on the train from London to Eastbourne, Mahon revealed that he had not done so, and that he had no intention of emigrating with her. Kaye became distraught. The quarrel continued at the bungalow, where an enraged Kaye:

" . . . suddenly picked up a weapon — a coal axe — and threw it at me. It struck me on the shoulder and glanced off and hit the door of the bedroom, breaking the shaft. We were then in the sitting-room. I felt appalled at the fury she showed and realized suddenly how strong the girl was.

She followed up the throw by dashing at me and clutching at my face and neck. In sheer desperation and fright I closed with her, doing my best to fight back and loosen her hold. We struggled, and eventually, in the course of the struggle, we fell over an easy chair, and Miss Kaye's head came in violent contact with a round iron cauldron.

At this time we were in the front sitting-room. The coal cauldron was at the side of the fireplace in the front sitting-room.

My body of course being on top when she fell, her hold relaxed a bit, and she lay apparently stone dead. The events of the next few seconds I cannot remember except as a nightmare of horror, for I saw blood begin to issue from Miss Kaye's head where she had struck the cauldron. I did my utmost to revive her. I simply could not say at the time whether I strangled her, or whether she died of the fall.

By this time the excitement of the struggle and the fright and the blows I had received had reduced me to a condition of nervous exhaustion, and as a realization of the terrible position flooded my brain, I think my mind was at the breaking strain. I think I wandered or sat down in the garden bordering on madness. Eventually I came back to the bungalow and pulled the body of Miss Kaye into the second bedroom where the trunk was, where I placed it gently down, covering it with her fur coat and placing underneath her head various clothing."

* * *

At this stage, Mahon had not been charged with murder, and he may have imagined that his successive statements about the quarrel and the accident at the bungalow would be believed. However, Detective Chief Inspector Savage quickly made the position clear: in his mind, Mahon was a murderer. Mahon would now be charged with murder, and was moved to Cannon Row police station.

Savage's next step was to call Sir Bernard Spilsbury. Sir Bernard Spilsbury can be described as a "celebrity pathologist" (or the "prince of pathology" as Savage referred to him). At a time when forensic science was developing rapidly, Spilsbury appeared as an expert witness in many high-profile murder cases. His name was widely known amongst the British public, who devoured newspaper reports of murder investigations.

Spilsbury arrived at the Crumbles early on the morning of Sunday 4 May, together with his assistant, Hilda Bainbridge. News of a gruesome discovery at the bungalow had spread rapidly, and a crowd of onlookers had already gathered as Spilsbury, Bainbridge and Savage entered the bungalow.

Spilsbury put his on his white apron and rubber gloves. He and Bainbridge worked methodically through the bungalow. Nearly 1,000 fragments of human bone were collected from the fireplaces in the sitting room and dining room.

Spilsbury tried to fit bones together like a jigsaw, but some were beyond identification. Other parts of Kaye's remains could be identified. Kaye's left shoulder and part of her chest were in the trunk in the bedroom: on her shoulder there was a bruise, seemingly caused by a heavy blow. Spilsbury also found a large section of abdominal wall, various organs in tact, parts of Kaye's hands, a tibia, a right femur, and a left radius. However, the head and upper part of Kaye's neck were completely missing. Spilsbury was later reported as saying that, in his long career in pathology, Kaye's remains in the Crumbles bungalow were the most gruesome he had ever worked with.

* * *

Percy Savage told Spilsbury that Mahon claimed to have disposed of Kaye's head by burning it in the sitting room fireplace. Initially, both Savage and Spilsbury were sceptical of this account, thinking it impossible to dispose of a head effectively in this way.

Under Spilsbury's supervision, the police carried out what Savage described as "a gruesome but interesting and necessary experiment". A large coal fire was lit in the fireplace in the bungalow's sitting room, and a sheep's head was placed on it. Within four hours, the sheep's head was reduced to a few charred and unrecognisable fragments. It appeared that Mahon was telling the truth about how he had disposed of Kaye's head.

Later, Mahon added a ghoulish detail to his story about the burning of the head. When he placed Emily Kaye's head on the coals in the grate, her blonde hair burnt first. Then the skin in her eyelids started to contract in the heat, pulling the eyes open. It was a hot, humid day and a violent thunder storm was raging over the bungalow. Mahon's nerve broke as he found himself being stared at by the eyes of his dead lover, whilst thunder and lightning broke overhead. He fled from the bungalow, and paced up and down the beach in the storm, until he steeled himself enough to return to the task of disposing of Kaye's remains.

* * *

An unexpected innovation in police methods resulted from the search of the Crumbles bungalow — the "murder bag". Spilsbury expressed astonishment that Savage had been sifting through Emily Kaye's remains with his bare hands, and pointed out in very direct terms the health risks to Savage of handling putrid flesh in this way. He asked Savage why he was not wearing rubber gloves, and was surprised when Savage replied that officers were not supplied with any. In fact, as Savage admitted, Scotland Yard officers lacked many forms of vital equipment:

> "We police officers not only had no rubber gloves, but we lacked many other things which were essential. If we wanted to preserve human hair on clothing or soil or dust on boots, we had to pick it up with our fingers and put it in a piece of paper. We had no tapes to measure distances, no compass to determine direction, no apparatus to take finger-prints, no first aid outfit, no instrument to find the depth of water, no magnifying glass. In fact, we had no appliances available for immediate use on the scene of a crime."

As a result of Spilsbury's intervention, the "murder bag" came into being. Detective Chief Inspector Savage made out a list of articles which a detective would find useful when investigating a murder: from then on, a "murder bag" was issued to Chief Inspectors.

* * *

On the evening of Sunday 4 May, Spilsbury and Bainbridge finished their work at the bungalow and returned to London. It was now getting dark, but there were still hundreds of sight-seers gathered along the coast road opposite the bungalow.

Spilsbury took with him all of the remains which he had collected. Back in London, in a room in the pathology department of Bart's hospital, Spilsbury began to put together the collection of flesh and bones. Working throughout the night, Spilsbury assembled Kaye's shoulder, chest, abdominal wall, surviving organs, and parts of her limbs.

He concluded that Emily Kaye had been between one and three months pregnant. Although unable to give a cause of death, Spilsbury was positive that Kaye had not died in the way that Mahon suggested, on the grounds that a fatal fall on the cauldron would have inflicted far more damage to it.

Police continued to look for body parts, in case more of Emily Kaye's remains could be found. A major search operation of the Crumbles and surrounding areas was mounted. There was some excitement when bones and a dental plate were found at a brickyard in Pevensey, but the bones turned out not to be human. Unconnected with the search for Kaye's remains, a human leg was found on Wimbledon Common. Spilsbury was able to confirm that, although the leg was a woman's, it did not belong to Emily Kaye. Oddly, the true owner of the leg was never identified.

* * *

With Emily Kaye lying partly re-assembled on a pathology table at Bart's hospital, the police faced the job of checking Mahon's story in detail.

Percy Savage worked with Inspectors Hall and Sprackling, going through Mahon's statement. They were able to piece together the events of the previous ten months. What they found was that, in some cases, Mahon had told the truth; however, in other areas — some of which were crucial to his claim of innocence — Mahon had lied.

Police found that Emily Kaye was a confident, popular woman. Through a combination of hard work and investment ability, she had built up a sizeable financial portfolio, worth something in the region of £600 (about £35,500 in today's money). She lived in the Green Cross Club, a residential club in Guildford Street, Bloomsbury, and had an active social life. When Kaye found out that another woman living at the Green Cross Club knew some of Mahon's business acquaintances, she suggested that Mahon should use a false name when visiting her there. As a result, when in Guildford Street, Mahon became 'Derek Patterson' — or 'Pat'.

Mahon was willing to fleece Emily Kaye for money. She dipped heavily into her investments, giving Mahon about £400 (approximately £23,500 in today's money). Mahon later claimed that some of this money was the result of currency speculation by Kaye, to which he had contributed funds. However, there was no evidence to support this.

* * *

On 4 April, Mahon saw an advertisement in the *Daily Telegraph* for a furnished bungalow on the coast, being offered to let on a short term basis. The next day, calling himself 'Mr. Waller' he went down to Eastbourne and, after being shown over the Officer's House, agreed to rent it for eight weeks, starting from 11 April. Mahon told the agent who showed him round, a Mr. Muir, that he was connected with the British Empire Exhibition, which was due to open at Wembley on 23 April. He also told Muir that he normally lived in a hotel in London, but that he wanted the bungalow because his wife needed rest and quiet.

At the same time, Emily Kaye started packing up her life in London — clearly in the expectation that after the 'love experiment', the couple would go to Paris and then to South Africa. She gave up her room in Guildford Street and bought a large quantity of French francs. She also wrote to her married sister, telling her that she was engaged to a man called 'Derek Patterson' or 'Pat', who was going to take a job in South Africa. According to Kaye, 'Pat' wanted her to go with him, and they would be married when they arrived there.

On Monday 7 April, Emily Kaye left London for good and took a room at the Kenilworth Court Hotel in Eastbourne. Mahon was due to arrive a few days later, so that the 'love experiment' could begin.

* * *

On Thursday 10 April, Mahon was at home in Richmond with his wife. That evening, he went for a walk near Richmond Park, and had a chance encounter with a 32 year old woman called Ethel Duncan. Mahon introduced himself as 'Pat'. Mahon clearly had a relaxed and easy manner, making Ethel Duncan confident enough to engage in conversation with a complete stranger.

It was a rainy night, and apparently Ethel, who was out of work and lived with her sister in Isleworth, was in a low mood. 'Pat' told Ethel that he was a married man, but that his marriage was on the rocks (he put this in suitably dramatic terms, describing his marriage as a 'tragedy.')

Before they parted, Mahon asked Ethel whether she would have dinner with him. Ethel felt suitably enthused by this invitation to give Mahon her address. "You will probably be hearing from me next Wednesday," said Mahon, as he started his journey on foot back to Richmond.

For a man who was trying to exit an awkward relationship, this was an extraordinary move. Mahon now had a wife waiting for him at home, a lover waiting for him in Eastbourne, and a woman waiting to be contacted with a dinner invitation. One suspects that Mahon was a man who enjoyed danger, or at least got a strange thrill from getting himself into and out of tricky situations.

On Saturday 12 April, the day on which the 'love experiment' was due to start, Mahon went into a shop in Victoria Street, London, and bought a large kitchen knife and an eight-inch meat saw.

Carrying his knife and saw in a bag (the bag which was later found at Waterloo station), Mahon caught the train to Eastbourne and met Emily Kaye. After dinner at the Sussex Hotel, the pair took a taxi to the bungalow, where they spent the next few days. On Sunday 13 April, a neighbour in the Coastguard Cottages saw Mahon and Kaye walking arm-in-arm on the beach.

Mahon killed Emily Kaye either on Monday 14 April or Tuesday 15 April. We do not know exactly how her death occurred, as we only have Mahon's story that she died when she caught her head on a coal scuttle. It seems feasible to imagine that Mahon and Kaye quarrelled, although nobody can say with certainty that Mahon killed her during an argument.

The fact that Mahon took such care to dispose of Emily Kaye's head and upper neck suggests that this was where the fatal wounds were to be found: he may have struck her, stabbed her, or strangled her (or some combination of these). Mahon had two knives at his disposal — the cook's knife which he bought in London, and a carving knife which was already in the bungalow — as well as an axe which was also already at the bungalow. In addition, it is possible that Kaye did fall during a struggle and hit her head, although, as we have seen, Sir Bernard Spilsbury took the view that a fall on the coal scuttle was not the cause of death.

There is no reason to disbelieve Mahon's own account of what happened after Kaye's death: he took Kaye's body into a bedroom and covered her with a fur coat.

On 15 April, Mahon sent a telegram to Edith Duncan: "Charing Cross seven tomorrow. Sure. Pat." The next day, he took a taxi to Eastbourne station, in time to catch the 4.30 p.m. train to London. He met Edith Duncan at Charing Cross station; Mahon and Duncan then went for dinner at a restaurant at Victoria Station.

Mahon told Duncan that he was using a bungalow on the coast which belonged to a friend. Without any irony, given what had just happened there, Mahon even described the bungalow as "rather a charming place". Mahon (or 'Pat' as Edith thought of him) wondered if Edith would like to join him there for an Easter holiday? Edith Duncan was clearly somewhat taken with Mahon, and she agreed.

Mahon spent the night at the Grosvenor Hotel at Victoria Station, before returning to Eastbourne. On Thursday 17 April, he sent her a telegram reading "Meet train as arranged". He also sent her £4, in the form of a telegraphic money order.

Obviously, Mahon had to ensure that Emily Kaye's body had been suitably dealt with before Edith Duncan arrived in Eastbourne. By Mahon's own account, he started by sawing Emily Kaye's legs off, but then found that he could not get the rest of the body in the trunk without taking the head off.

Mahon and Edith Duncan's Easter holiday by the seaside started on Good Friday, 18 April, by which time Emily Kaye's newly severed legs, torso and head were stored in a bedroom at the bungalow. Duncan caught the 11.15 a.m. train to Eastbourne. A pleasant day followed — lunch, a motor tour round the area known for its many beauty spots, followed by dinner at the Royal Hotel, Eastbourne. The pair then took a taxi to the Crumbles.

That night Mahon and Edith Duncan shared the same bed which Mahon and Emily Kaye had shared a few nights before. Despite the fact that the remains of Emily Kaye were in the next door bedroom, Duncan later reported that Mahon appeared to be quite normal and was in good spirits. She noticed that there were various items belonging to a woman in the bungalow — some cosmetics on a dressing table, a tortoiseshell hair brush, and a pair of high-heeled shoes on the floor — but Mahon told her that these were his wife's, adding that his wife had stayed at the bungalow the week before.

Briefly, Edith Duncan caught a glimpse of the trunk in which some of Emily Kaye's dismembered remains were stored. This was whilst Mahon was working on the door of the neighbouring bedroom: he explained that the door had to be fixed securely with screws, because a friend had left some valuable books in the room.

On the Saturday of the Easter weekend, Mahon took Edith Duncan to Eastbourne. She spent the day alone there and Mahon went on to a race meeting at Plumpton, north of Brighton. It was whilst at Plumpton that he was spotted by a mutual acquaintance who reported the sighting to Mahon's wife.

How to dispose of Emily Kaye's remains was very much on Mahon's mind. Mahon knew that it was necessary to get Emily Duncan away from Eastbourne. In order to achieve this, Mahon set up a ruse. He sent a telegram to the bungalow, addressed to himself: the telegram purported to be from a business acquaintance, and indicated that the sender wanted to see Mahon on Tuesday morning.

Mahon and Edith Duncan returned to the bungalow on the Saturday evening, and by the time that they arrived, the telegram had already been delivered. Mahon opened the telegram and told Duncan that he had been recalled to London.

Mahon and Duncan caught the train to London on the morning of Easter Monday. They spent the day together, having dinner at a West End restaurant, going to the music hall, and catching a late train back to Richmond. The pair parted at about midnight, Mahon returning to his wife for the night.

Later, Mahon was asked why he had brought Edith Duncan to the bungalow, given the gruesome secrets it contained. Mahon explained that he found it unbearable to be in the bungalow alone: "I should have gone stark raving mad if I had not had Miss Duncan with me," he said. "It was ghastly . . . The damn place was haunted; I wanted human company."

On Tuesday 22 April, Mahon returned to Eastbourne. Now he could start to dispose of the body. It was on the Tuesday that he burned Emily Kaye's head in the fire in the sitting room — to the dramatic accompaniment of a thunder storm overhead. Mahon found that a number of charred bones remained in the ashes of the fire, so he crushed these between his fingers and threw them over the wall at the back of the bungalow, hoping that they would disappear into the shingle. It seems reasonable to believe Mahon's own statement, that other remains were disposed of (after boiling) by throwing them out of the window of a moving train.

These cut up and boiled remains were carried in the bag which was deposited at Waterloo station. Mahon's scheme was to pick the bag up at Waterloo when he wanted to go down to the bungalow to collect more flesh for disposal.

* * *

The murder of Emily Kaye released Mahon — temporarily at least — from an otherwise insoluble predicament. At the beginning of April 1924, Mahon knew that he was trapped. He had taken a large amount of money from a woman who was emotionally dependent on him, and who was now putting pressure on him. It appears that Mahon did not want to leave his marriage — although he did not want to stay faithful within it either. It is unclear whether Mahon knew that Emily Kaye was pregnant but, if he did, this could only have added to the pressure.

In retrospect, it can be seen that Emily Kaye's own suggestions gave Mahon a way out of his predicament. The 'love experiment' provided Mahon with a suitably remote place to murder Kaye: for him, it was the place for a 'murder experiment'. Then, Kaye's plan to emigrate to South Africa provided Mahon with cover: when Emily Kaye disappeared, she would not be reported missing, because it would be assumed by her family and friends that she had sailed for South Africa.

Mahon had, in a sense, become a number of different people, who (he hoped) could not be connected. There was Patrick Mahon, a married man from Richmond; there was Derek Patterson (or 'Pat') the man who was having an affair with Emily Kaye; there was another 'Pat' — the man who had wined and dined Edith Duncan; and finally, there was 'Mr. Waller', the man who had rented an Eastbourne bungalow.

* * *

After being committed for trial at Hailsham police court, Patrick Mahon's trial began on 15 July 1924 at Lewes.

As the trial approached, the police were by no means confident that a verdict of guilty would be returned. Mahon might come over as a plausible witness, and his story of the 'quarrel which went wrong' might be believed.

Detective Chief Inspector Savage was in court for the trial, and what struck him forcefully was the effort which Mahon had put into his appearance:

"He wore a stylish blue lounge suit which had been specially ordered from his tailor at a cost of seven guineas, a soft collar, and tie. His hands were carefully manicured, and his face was tanned as though he had been enjoying a month's holiday at a sunny south coast resort. His bronzed complexion, however, was merely the result of a clever piece of deceit. In some way he had managed to procure a stain — tobacco juice was suggested — which he applied to his face to give it the appearance of honest robustness."

Another account of the trial reported that:

> "Mahon was looking considerably more healthy than at the police court proceedings shortly before. He seemed sunburnt and fat, although there was a striking contrast in the colour of his hands, which were pale and delicate. As a fact, Mahon had expressed a wish to obtain some chemical tan while in jail. His clear-cut handsome features radiated confidence."

However, despite the attention which he put into his appearance, Mahon did not manage to strike the right note when giving evidence. One observer noted that:

> "He was anxious to 'make a good impression' in court. He was overeager and obsequious, smiling round at the jury, nervously trying to please. But he succeeded in being merely irritating. He had a habit of replying 'Quite' to his counsel's questions. He was glib and unashamed as he told the story of the 'love experiment.' "

According to another account, Mahon:

> ". . . made a poor impression in the witness box. He is said to have been confident, almost to the end, that his looks and charm would spell-bind the jury and even Mr. Justice Avory. But his manner was either too jaunty or too dramatic."

The centre piece of Mahon's defence was his dramatic account of the quarrel over emigrating and the struggle in the sitting room. He described how the usually good-tempered Kaye had thrown an axe at him and behaved like "an infuriated tiger":

> "I became absolutely uneasy with fear and fright . . . with almost a last despairing throw I pushed her off and we both fell over the easy-chair to the left of the fireplace. Miss Kaye's head hit the cauldron, and I fell with her."

For most of the time, Mahon maintained his composure whilst giving evidence. However, when he came to the story of Emily

Kaye throwing the axe at him, he broke down in tears. During cross-examination by the prosecution counsel, Sir Henry Curtis Bennett, the strain became too much. Sweat started running down Mahon's forehead, and he had to wipe his eyes with a silk pocket handkerchief. He seemed to be shaking slightly, and looked as if he was about to feint. He was clearly so overcome that he was given permission to sit down.

A moment of high drama came during Mahon's account of how he disposed of Emily Kaye's remains. According to Mahon, the decision to burn and boil the remains was made when he found that the trunk was too full of body parts for the lid to close. Mr. Cassels, Mahon's defence counsel, then asked him:

"On the Tuesday you burned the head?"

As Mahon replied "That is so" a clap of thunder broke over the courtroom.

The sudden thunder unnerved Mahon, who shrank back and gripped the witness box: he was reported as cowering. It seemed as if the clap of thunder over Lewes brought back to him the moment when Emily Kaye's eyes were pulled open by the heat of the fire, and a thunderstorm broke over the bungalow.

There were other moments of drama. One juryman fainted, and another asked to be excused — it is unclear whether this was due to the gruesome nature of the evidence. When Ethel Duncan was asked to identify Mahon in the court room she cried "Oh, don't please!" and sobbed uncontrollably as she looked at Mahon.

* * *

The jury must have been transfixed by the story which was set out in front of them.

It seems likely that the story of how Mahon met Ethel Duncan and invited her to dinner, whilst his pregnant lover was waiting for him in Eastbourne, and his faithful wife was waiting for him at home, did not play in Mahon's favour.

One particular difficulty which Mahon faced concerned the knife and saw which he had bought on the first day of the 'love experiment'. As we have seen, when he made his statement at Scotland Yard, Mahon told Detective Chief Inspector Savage that he had bought these on 17 April — in other words, *after* Emily Kaye had died. However, police produced a receipt from the shop confirming that Mahon had bought them on 12 April — the first day of the 'love experiment'.

This discrepancy in dates significantly weakened Mahon's defence. Why had he bought a sharp cook's knife and a meat saw when Emily Kaye was still alive? The obvious implication was that Mahon had gone to Eastbourne knowing that he would need them to dispose of Emily Kaye's body.

In relation to the cook's knife, Mahon tried to resist this implication by saying that he had not used this knife to cut up Emily Kaye: instead, he had used a carving knife which was already in one of the draws in the bungalow. The reason he gave for the choice of knife was bizarre, and cannot have sounded very convincing to the jury. According to Mahon, Emily Kaye had handled the cook's knife whilst she was still alive and so, for sentimental reasons, he preferred not to cut her up with it. Mahon's story was further undermined when Sir Bernard Spilsbury gave evidence that the carving knife in the bungalow would not have been sharp enough to cut through skin.

* * *

Mahon was unlucky in the choice of judge for the trial. Mr Justice Avory was a 72 year old with a reputation as a "hanging judge". Most of Avory's legal career had been during the Victorian era, and he brought a Victorian strictness to the task of presiding over a court. Avory was often unsympathetic and sarcastic to defendants. His nickname amongst lawyers was the "acid drop", and he was once described as "scrawny-necked, thin-lipped and fearsome."

During the trial it was clear that Mr Justice Avory had taken against Mahon. When Mahon described the quarrel with Emily Kaye, Mr. Justice Avory interrupted him sharply: "We want to know what happened, not what you thought and what you imagined, but what happened."

When Mahon described his feelings on realising that Kaye was dead — "it suddenly dawned on me what a horrible thing it was, she was there and dead. I think the realization of the fact that she was dead flooded my mind . . . " — Mr Justice Avory made another sharp interruption:"You were asked what you did, not all this imagination. You were asked what you did."

At the end of the trial, Mr Justice Avory's summing-up was deeply unsympathetic to Mahon. Avory told the jury:

"In asking yourselves whether his subsequent conduct is consistent with any view that this was a death happening without his intention and desire, you have to look at the evidence of his taking this other woman to the bungalow on Good Friday, sleeping with her in the very room which he had occupied with the deceased woman for the three nights, and actually taking the precaution, before she arrives there, to go there himself and cut the head off, in order that he may pack it in the trunk out of sight.

Is that conduct which you would expect of a man who feels any kind of remorse at a death which he neither desired nor intended? He took the trouble to burn the head and collect the bones. Why this trouble?

Having burnt the head, as he said, for six hours, he then took the precaution — mark this — of collecting such bones or such remains of bones as were still left from the fire and breaking them up into small fragments with his fingers and thumb and casting them on the beach where they could not possibly be recognized or identified.

Why take this meticulous care to destroy every fragment of the skull, unless it were for the purpose of concealing the injuries on the head which might afford conclusive testimony to what had really happened on that night, instead of a mere fall on this rickety old cauldron?"

* * *

The jury's deliberations were swift, taking only about 45 minutes. They found Mahon guilty.

When Mahon was asked if he had anything to say as to why judgment of death should not be pronounced, he held himself straight and looked directly at Mr Justice Avory. In a clear voice which suggested controlled anger he said:

"I feel too conscious of the bitterness and unfairness of the summing-up which you have just uttered to say anything except that I am not guilty of murder."

After the death sentence was passed, Mr. Justice Avory revealed that Mahon had a number of previous convictions, a fact which had been withheld from the jury during the trial. The most serious of these convictions related to a bank robbery in 1916. The robbery had gone wrong and, during it, Mahon violently attacked a woman with a hammer. Mr. Justice Avory told Mahon:

"The jury have arrived at their conclusion, without knowing anything of your past life. They do not know that you have already suffered a term of penal servitude for a crime of violence. There can be no doubt that you deliberately designed the death of this woman."

Mahon appealed against his conviction, partly on the grounds that Mr Justice Avory had misdirected the jury. The appeal was dismissed, and Patrick Mahon was executed on 2 September 1924.

Mahon's executioner was Thomas Pierrepoint, from the well-known family of hangmen (Thomas and Henry Pierrepoint were brothers and both were hangmen; Henry's son, Albert, later took up the family profession, becoming the most prolific executioner in British history).

The procedure for execution involved placing the feet of the man about to be hung on two chalk marks on a wooden platform. With this done, as swiftly as possible, the hangman would move a lever, causing the platform to swing away from under the man's feet.

As he sensed that Pierrepoint was about to pull the lever, Mahon moved forward in an attempt to place his feet on the solid floor in front of the platform. However, Mahon did not manage to get a firm foot-hold, and his body lurched backwards, until he fell and the jerk of the rope broke his spine at the neck.

In most cases, the *post mortem* of an executed man was a fairly perfunctory affair, given that the cause of death was obvious. However, for reasons which are not clear, Sir Bernard Spilsbury decided that he wanted to perform the *post mortem* on Mahon, and to do so with more rigour than normally followed an execution.

Standard procedure following an execution was to open the body in the area of the neck, where the fracture in the spine was to be found. However, Spilsbury opened Mahon's body up with a much larger 'top to bottom' incision. Spilsbury also spent about an hour examining Mahon's brain, even removing part of it to send to the coroner. It is unclear what scientific information this produced. Spilsbury reported that Mahon's spine was broken between the 4th and 5th cervical vertebrae, and that this was accompanied by considerable movement between the 6th and 7th vertebrae.

Mahon's wife, Jessie Hannah Mahon, never remarried. She died in in 1974 in Surrey.

2 The Camberwell Triple Murder

* * *

89, Church Road, Leyton, East London
22, Wyndham Road, Camberwell, South London
November-December 1902

* * *

On a cold Tuesday morning just before Christmas, a coal carter was driving down a quiet road in Leyton, when he heard the sound of breaking glass. The sound came from a nearby house. Peering towards the house, the carter realised that the glass panel in the front door had just been smashed. As he watched, a bloodstained hand appeared through the hole in the glass, before disappearing back into the house.

The carter pulled up his horse and cart and rushed up the path to the front door. Inside, a man was groaning and shouting "Murder! Murder!". The carter put his hand through the splintered glass panel, reached for the latch and opened the door.

Lying in the hall in front of him was a middle-aged man. His head was covered in blood, and he was mumbling whilst gesturing up the stairs, as if warning that danger was to be found up there. Then, he collapsed into unconsciousness.

Running back into the street, the coal carter summoned help from neighbours and passers-by. Shortly afterwards, a policeman arrived, and was just in time to see a man trying to escape through the small garden at the rear of the house. The policeman grabbed the would-be escapee and wrestled him to the ground.

With the man in custody, a message was sent by telegraph from Leyton police station to the Divisional Criminal Investigation Department (C.I.D.) at Bethnal Green. The message contained enough details to convince the C.I.D. Inspector at Bethnal Green that this might be a case of attempted murder. Two officers — Detective Sergeant Burgess and Detective Constable Percy Savage — were dispatched to Leyton immediately, with the instruction "Get on to it as quickly as possible."

Detective Constable Savage had only joined the C.I.D in the previous year. He thought that Bethnal Green was a good training ground for a young detective because, as he put it, "all sorts of criminals were to be found there". However, as he made his way to Leyton, what Savage did not know was that he was about to become involved in investigating a grisly triple murder.

* * *

Burgess and Savage arrived at Leyton police station, to find the man who had tried to escape from the house sitting in the station's charge room.

A uniformed officer gave Burgess and Savage a crisp summary of events. The man in custody was called Edgar Edwards, although little else was known about him. The injured man, John Garland, was still alive, although critically ill at the nearby West Ham hospital. Edwards had hit Garland repeatedly on the head with a heavy metal weight. For reasons which were not yet clear, the weight had been wrapped in paper and tied up with red tape.

In the charge room, Detective Constable Savage looked at Edwards intently. He was tall and powerfully built. As the uniformed officer recited the facts of the assault and the arrest, Savage was struck by the fact that Edwards remained curiously detached, reacting without emotion or surprise. Savage also thought that there was a strange expression in Edwards' eyes.

When Edwards smiled, Savage could not make out whether Edwards was simply smiling pleasantly or with contempt.

Edwards gave his side of the story. He explained the he and Garland had been arguing about a boxing match. When the argument became heated, Garland had tried to hit Edwards. Acting in self-defence, Edwards then hit back with the metal weight. This caused Garland to stumble down the stairs, where he injured himself by hitting his head.

This struck Savage as an unlikely explanation. As well as being strongly-built, Edwards was younger than Garland — did it make sense that he would use a heavy weight in self-defence? In addition, Edwards didn't have a scratch on him, or any other sign of injury — where was the evidence that Garland had attacked him?

The detectives asked Edwards for more information about himself. At this point, Edwards became strangely withdrawn, clearly not wanting to give much away. He explained that he had only lived at 89, Church Road — the house where the attack took place — for two or three weeks. Garland had come to the house in order to discuss business. Edwards explained his reluctance to give any further information by saying that he did not want his family to get mixed up in the affair.

Edwards' clothes were searched. In one of his pockets, officers found a pawnbroker's ticket, made out in the name of 'Darby'. More pawnbroker's tickets, together with visiting cards, bearing the name 'Darby' or 'William Darby' were found when the police searched 89, Church Road that evening. These showed that Darby's address was 22, Wyndham Road, Camberwell.

The obvious conclusion was that Edwards had been trying to conceal his identity. Was Edwards really William Darby? However, Edwards denied this emphatically. In a calm, unruffled way he repeated that his name was Edwards, explaining that he was acting on behalf of Darby, a friend who had been interested in buying a business from John Garland.

The search of 89, Church Road did not reveal any other clues. The house was sparsely furnished, and the furniture was placed in a rather random and untidy way. The detectives wondered if this was a sign that Edwards was a single man living alone. After examining the stairs for signs of a struggle, the house was locked up and placed under guard.

The police visited 22, Wyndham Road, Camberwell next. 22, Wyndham Road turned out to be a small grocery business run out of a corner shop. The shop was locked up, with the shutters pulled across the windows.

Neighbours told the police that, until recently, the shop had been run by William and Beatrice Darby. William and Beatrice were a couple in their 20s, and had been married for about a year. They had a three month old daughter, Ethel. At the beginning of December, without any warning, the Darbys had sold their grocery business and gone away — no one knew where. After the Darbys left, the shop re-opened, with a new owner. However, the new owner only stayed for just over a week, before closing the shop and disappearing.

The mystery of who the Darbys were, and what had happened to them, only began to resolve itself after Christmas. The police discovered that Beatrice Darby had a sister, Elizabeth Baldwin. Baldwin lived nearby, in Sangley Road, Catford. When the police contacted her, despite trying not to give her any grounds for alarm, it was clear that she was already very anxious about her sister. She told Detective Constable Savage that she was certain that something dreadful had happened to the Darby family.

Elizabeth Baldwin had last heard from her sister at the end of November. Beatrice Darby had written to Elizabeth, asking if she would like to visit Wyndham Road in order to see Ethel, the baby. Elizabeth duly arrived in Camberwell on 3 December, but was surprised to find an unknown man and a woman working behind the counter of the shop. When she asked to see her sister, she was told that the Darby family had sold the business, and that the new owner of the business would be at the shop shortly.

As promised, the new owner, a man, arrived a little while later. Elizabeth Baldwin stayed at the shop for an hour quizzing him. Baldwin said that she could not understand the shop being sold so quickly, but the man replied "Oh, I first negotiated with Mr. Darby on Saturday morning; I was so satisfied with the business, I have paid £30 on deposit, and if Mr. Darby comes in I will settle with him then". He told Elizabeth Baldwin that William Darby was expected at the shop at any moment to finalise the sale by collecting the balance of the money owed to him. He also assured her that the Darby family had gone away with their daughter and were staying with friends — although he did not know where.

Baldwin noticed that the man's face had gone a little red when she was introduced as Beatrice Darby's sister. Otherwise, she found him pleasant and affable, later reporting that "I did not notice any fear in his manner".

However, Elizabeth Baldwin was far from reassured — although, without further information, there was little that she could do. After waiting for a while in case her brother-in-law William turned up, she returned home, full of anxious uncertainty about what had really happened. Throughout the rest of December she hoped that her sister would write to her, but no letter came.

After Edwards' arrest, the police decided that it would be a good idea for Elizabeth Baldwin to visit his house in Leyton, in case this shed any light on the matter. She did so on 29 December, accompanied by Detective Constable Savage and Detective Sergeant Melville.

When she entered the front room at 89, Church Road, she got a chilling shock: the furniture in the house was her sister's. Looking through the house, further shocks followed: in an upstairs cupboard, there was a woman's coat and hat, which Elizabeth Baldwin identified as belonging to her sister. She told Savage that her sister would have taken the coat and hat with her if she really had gone away.

After a pause, she looked at Savage with a terrified expression, and whispered: "They've been murdered." Elizabeth Baldwin found it hard to contain her emotions. In tears, she walked restlessly up and down the room. Then, looking towards the back garden, she announced dramatically: "That's where their bodies are. I feel certain of it."

Baldwin's suspicions were reported back to the Inspector at Bethnal Green, who gave the instruction that the garden should be dug up. "If you find nothing no harm will be done" he told Savage. "And if you do find something . . . "

The dig took place the next day. After about an hour, a police officer found a soft patch of earth about half way down the garden, close to a corrugated iron fence. Digging down, he found six sacks and a bundle between four and five feet (1.2 to 1.5 metres) below the surface. The Divisional police surgeon, the unfortunately named Dr. Jekyll, was then called to examine the contents of the sacks and the bundle. Jekyll's account gives a clear picture of what was inside:

"I saw six sacks containing the dismembered bodies of a man and woman; the heads and limbs had been cut off. I also saw the body of a child, which was intact. The heads were quite recognisable. The cause of death was due to injury to the heads in the cases of the man and woman, and in the case of the child to strangulation — there was a handkerchief tied tightly round its neck.

There were extensive fractures to the skulls of the man and woman. There had been three or four blows delivered. The face of the woman had been smashed in, and there had also been a blow on the back of each of their heads. The serious blows had been struck from the front. The bodies had been dismembered by means of a saw."

* * *

News that three bodies had been found turned the case into a murder investigation. Senior detectives were called to the scene, and the Assistant-Commissioner in charge of the C.I.D., Sir Edward Henry (today remembered as the man who championed the introduction of finger-prints in Scotland Yard) took overall charge.

Until now, the shop at 22, Wyndham Road had not been searched. Searching the shop became a priority task. When Detective Constable Savage, together with other officers, arrived at the shop, they found the interior completely bare. All of the stock had been removed and there was no furniture left in the living quarters over the shop.

What was also obvious was a considerable amount of blood. Blood had oozed through the upstairs floor boards, leaving a large stain on the shop ceiling below. On the first floor there were large blood stains, particularly in the front bedroom and on the landing.

Dr. Arthur Luff, a forensic pathologist from St. Mary's Hospital, visited the house. In the upstairs front room, Luff found:

". . . several blood stains which had been projected from a living artery or arteries . . . there were also several underneath the mantelshelf . . . there were several bloodstains at two different levels on the wall between the fireplace and the window, which also had all been projected from an artery or arteries during life . . . on the window sash, and on the lower part of the window blind, there were bloodstains, and there were a few bloodstains on one of the lowest panes of the window and the lowest part of the blind — there were two very large stains on the floor, one in front of the fireplace, and the other in front of the left window."

The trail of blood continued on the landing:

". . . outside the door at the head of the staircase there is a small landing with three doors opening from it. On the outer side of the door of the front room there were several blood stains which had been projected from arteries or an artery, during life — on the outer side of the door of the bedroom, there were also some blood stains, which had been projected from an artery or arteries during life, and which had been slightly washed."

Officers also found a blood-stained 5.5 pounds (2.5 kg) metal weight which had been left lying on the floor. It was a sash-weight — of the type used in the closing mechanism of windows or doors — and a single human hair was embedded in the blood which had congealed on it.

When the bodies of the Darby family were discovered on 30 December, Edwards was still on remand for the assault on Garland. The discovery of the bodies meant that he was now charged with murder. When charged, Edwards replied "My dear sir, I know nothing about it."

* * *

Over the days which followed, using statements from a variety of sources, detectives were able to piece together what had happened. It was necessary somehow to connect the dismembered bodies found in Church Road, Leyton with the bloodstained scenes at the shop in Wyndham Road, Camberwell.

Police discovered that William Darby's grocery business had been struggling. As a result, towards the end of 1902, he advertised it for sale for £50 (equivalent to nearly £6,000 in today's money). For this, a buyer would receive all of the stock in the shop and the goodwill associated with the business; the buyer would also take over the tenancy of the shop, which was rented from James Knight, an ironmonger from the Camberwell Road

Edgar Edwards saw that the business was for sale, and started negotiating with William Darby. He also made arrangements for two old acquaintances, a couple called James and Alice Goodwin, to run the shop.

Although he had not seen the Goodwins for about a year, on 28 November Edwards paid a surprise visit to their home near the Elephant and Castle. Edwards announced that he was planning to buy a shop, and that he would like the Goodwins to work in it. James Goodwin suffered from an abnormally curved spine, which limited the kind of work he could do. It seems likely that James and Alice Goodwin were grateful for the offer of employment: they certainly accepted it readily. Having got the Goodwins' agreement that they would run the shop, Edwards added a special request, asking James Goodwin to buy a sash-weight.

Edwards returned to the Goodwins house on Sunday 30 November, and spent the whole day there. He appears to have been a demanding guest. He arrived at 8.30 a.m., ate breakfast, lunch and tea, and stayed late reading the newspaper. Then, at a point when he might reasonably be expected to leave, Edwards announced that he had missed the last bus — the horse-drawn omnibus to Victoria Park — and asked if he could stay the night. Alice Goodwin obligingly made a bed up for him in the front room.

The next morning, Alice provided Edwards with breakfast and a fresh shirt collar (this was the era when men wore shirts with detachable collars). Edwards then complained that he had no money on him and asked Alice to take his umbrella to a local pawnbrokers. Alice did this, pledging the umbrella at a pawnbrokers called Thompsons, in East Street: she returned with 1s 6d, which she gave to Edwards. James Goodwin also handed Edwards the sash-weight which he had bought, as requested.

Armed with a small amount of cash and a sash-weight, Edwards set off for Camberwell. He told the Goodwins that he should be able to conclude the purchase of the shop that morning, and instructed them to meet him on the corner of Wyndham Road at 11.30 a.m..

Edwards arrived in Wyndham Road sometime after 11 a.m., and was welcomed by William Darby who, one imagines, was relieved at having found a buyer for his struggling grocery business.

The two men went upstairs. Edwards was carrying the sash-weight, but had wrapped it in white paper, tied round with red tape — the kind of tape used to tie up bundles of legal documents. Edwards' aim was to disguise the weight, and make it look as if he was carrying the deed of transfer, the formal document which was necessary for the sale of the business.

When the two men were on the landing, Edwards launched a ferocious attack on William Darby. Standing behind him, Edwards struck Darby on the head with the weight a number of times, fracturing his skull. Beatrice Darby heard the commotion upstairs, and ran up to see what was going on: Edwards attacked her with the weight, fracturing her skull and inflicting horrific facial injuries. Whilst her parents were being attacked upstairs, Ethel, the baby, was downstairs in the kitchen. After attacking William and Beatrice Darby, Edwards went downstairs and strangled Ethel, before taking her body upstairs to join those of her parents.

The murders appear to have taken Edwards longer than he expected. Despite arranging to meet the Goodwins at 11.30 a.m., he did not emerge from the shop until just after noon. When the Goodwins saw him in the street they noticed that he had his sleeves rolled up and was wearing a white apron. Edwards apologised for his lateness, explaining that "he had been running about settling the matter with Mr. Darby".

Edwards took the Goodwins into the shop, and asked them what they thought of it. James Goodwin replied that he thought it was alright, but that Camberwell was a rough neighbourhood. There is some irony in this: Goodwin, obviously, had no idea that the bodies of three recently murdered people lay upstairs.

By 2 p.m. the shop was trading again, with James Goodwin happily serving customers. Edwards had dragged the bodies of the

Darby family into a bedroom upstairs and locked the door. He told the Goodwins that on no account should they go upstairs. The Goodwins obeyed this instruction to the letter. In the shop, the only hint of the carnage upstairs was the blood which oozed through the floor boards and stained the ceiling below: however, the Goodwins claimed not to have noticed the stain.

With the shop up and running, Edwards took the opportunity to raise some cash. He found Darby's gold watch and chain, which he pawned for £7 10s. More of William Darby's property, including two gold rings, was pawned over the days which followed. Edwards also gave the Goodwins 30 shillings, telling James Goodwin to get some decent clothes to make him look "a little respectable". James had previously taken his best clothes to the pawnbrokers, so he used the money to redeem them; at the same time, on Edwards' instructions, he retrieved the umbrella which he had pawned only that morning. More of the Darby's possessions were used to raise cash over the coming days.

A period of seeming normality followed. The Goodwins ran the shop for the next ten days, following a set routine. Edwards would unlock the shop at about 7.45 a.m., letting the Goodwins in. At closing time, 10 p.m., Edwards would come to lock the shop up. Several customers asked where the Darby family were, but they were told that the business was under new ownership and that the Darbys had moved on.

Edwards knew that the big problem facing him was how to dispose of the bodies of William, Beatrice and Ethel, which were now slowly decomposing upstairs. His solution was to find another property, with a garden which could be used as a burial ground.

At 10.30 a.m. on 3 December, Edwards went to the offices of Bassetts, a house letting agent in Lea Bridge Road. Edwards said that he would like to take over the tenancy of 89, Church Road, Leyton. In order to secure the tenancy, Edwards produced two forged references, which were typewritten, including the signatures. One of these forged references was in the name of William John Darby, and stated that Edwards had been a tenant of Darby's for nearly two years.

It seems also that Edwards saw a second opportunity in Church Road, Leyton — to commit another murder.

It may be that the surprise visit from Beatrice Darby's sister on 3 December spurred Edwards into action. On Friday 5 December Edwards started moving as much as possible out of the shop in Wyndham Road. Edwards hired a pony and cart: he was observed leaving Wyndham Road with the cart loaded up, returning with the cart empty nearly four hours later.

On Monday 8 December, he hired a pony and cart again. A witness saw Edwards and Goodwin loading the cart with two heavy sacks; Edwards returned some hours later with an empty cart. On Tuesday 9 December Edwards hired a van, which he loaded with furniture, a bath, two wooden boxes and a large tin trunk. Inside the bath, there was something under a cover.

By Wednesday 10 December, the remains of the Darby family, together with all of their furniture and belongings, had been taken to 89, Church Road, Leyton. It seems likely that the two adult bodies had already been dismembered, with their heads and limbs sawn off, in order to make them easier to transport.

Edwards now faced another problem. If Edwards had bought William Darby's grocery business in the proper way, Darby would have been required to get the approval of the shop's landlord. However, for obvious reasons, William Darby was now in no position to do this. In early December, the landlord turned up at the shop and pointed out that William Darby was in arrears on his rent, and that Edwards had no legal right to be at the shop. The landlord told Edwards that he would send the bailiffs in, a threat which was carried out on 10 December.

It is not clear whether this induced Edwards to abandon the shop, or whether he planned to do this in any case. Either way, on 10 December, he let the Goodwins in to the shop as normal, saying that he would be back at about 11 a.m.. He never returned. After the bailiffs arrived, the Goodwins were forced to cease trading, although Edwards did pay them a small amount of money to compensate for the sudden end of their brief career as shop-keepers.

* * *

89, Church Road, Leyton now became Edwards' centre of operations. On the evening of 10 December, Edwards invited a woman called Sarah Summers to the house in Leyton — rather bizarrely, considering that the house now contained three corpses. Edwards and Summers had been in a relationship some years previously, and had a child together — a boy, Charlie, who was now 14 years of age. Since Charlie's birth, Edwards had drifted in and out of Summers' life, and had been out of contact for long periods.

Edwards had got in touch with Summers out of the blue a fortnight before, having not seen her for about five years. He told her about his plans to buy a grocery business. He also invited her to visit the shop although, rather ominously, he emphasised that there was "one room we should not be able to go into for some time".

In the end, Summers never went to the shop, but instead visited him in Church Road, Leyton, where she and Edwards spent the night of 10 December. When Edwards was showing Summers over the house, she started to go towards a small upstairs back room. However, Edwards warned her "Come out, there is nothing there for you to see". This suggests that, as he had done at Camberwell, Edwards had set aside one room to store the Darby's remains.

The police considered that Edwards may have intended to kill Sarah Summers. However, she left Church Road safely on the morning of 11 December.

Edwards now faced the task of burial. He started by paying a neighbour to dig the back garden over — presumably, to disguise the fact that a triple burial was about to take place in it. Edwards then dug the burial hole. Sophia Frear, the next door neighbour at 91, Church Road, was standing at a bedroom window overlooking the back garden, when she was intrigued to see Edwards digging a hole in his garden so deep that only the top of his head could be seen. The next day, she noticed that the hole had been filled in.

With the evidence of his first three murders safely below ground, Edwards was ready to move on to his next one.

Edwards' intended victim this time was another shopkeeper — John Garland. Garland and his wife ran a grocer's shop on the corner of Jodrell Road, Victoria Park, a few miles south west of Leyton. Garland had advertised his business for sale, and Edwards made known his interest in purchasing it. The two men agreed to meet to discuss business.

In preparation for meeting Garland, Edwards got a sash-weight and wrapped it in paper. Just as he had done before the Camberwell murders, he asked an old acquaintance to buy the sash-weight for him. It appears that Edwards was a creature of habit.

Garland arrived at Church Road on the morning of 23 December. The men spent several hours talking. Then, when they were upstairs, Edwards mounted a surprise attack. According to Garland, Edwards:

". . . gave me a very severe blow — it almost knocked the senses out of me. It was followed by a number of blows rained upon me while I was on the ground. In another moment he might have killed me. Towards the end of the attack he tried to force a handkerchief or cloth into my mouth. He was almost exhausted by the force of his own blows; he began to show signs of fatigue."

This, of course, brings the story back to where we started. The attack on Garland led to Edwards' arrest, and began the whole process of unravelling what had happened at Wyndham Road, Camberwell.

* * *

Who was Edgar Edwards? Police discovered that 'Edgar Edwards' was an alias — Edwards had, in fact, been born 'Edwin Owen'. Throughout his life Edwin Owen used a series of false names. He was at various times, 'Edwin Smith', 'Henry George Freeman', and 'Harry Glanville'. His use of aliases must sometimes have been confusing to those around him: even though the Goodwins knew him as 'Harry Glanville', he told them that he planned to trade at Wyndham Road under the name 'William Thomas Louden'. Edwin Owen was charged with the murder of the Darby family under the name 'Edgar Edwards' and, to avoid confusion, we will revert to that name for the remainder of his story.

Edgar Edwards was the middle child of a family of seven children from Southwark. His father, John Owen, was said to be an alcoholic, who diverted scarce family funds to support his drinking habit (although Edgar remained loyal to his father, and later denied vehemently that his father had a drinking problem, regarding the suggestion of alcoholism as a slur on his reputation).

Edwards had a number of convictions. In 1888, at about the time that his son Charlie was born, he received an 18 month sentence for stealing watches. Barely two years later, he was sentenced to seven years penal servitude (a sentence normally involving hard labour) for burglary and receiving stolen goods. After release, he rented a shop in Bow Road, but this ended in a sentence of five years penal servitude: Edwards hired a pony and cart from a nearby publican, and disappeared with the mahogany fixtures from the shop. The idea of taking over a shop and removing its contents appears to have appealed to Edwards, given that he repeated this *modus operandi* in Camberwell, and may have been planning to repeat it in Victoria Park.

* * *

Edwards' trial opened at the Old Bailey in February 1903. Given Edwards' history of violence, during the trial he was always guarded by at least five warders.

Edwards' behaviour during the trial was striking. He started by displaying indifference to what was going on around him. He wore *pince-nez* spectacles — the sort which balance on the bridge of the wearer's nose without any side-arms for support — and, as he stood in the dock, Edwards took off his *pince-nez* and started to polish them. After the indictment had been read over to him, he was asked whether he pleaded guilty or not guilty. However, Edwards refused to reply, and simply continued to polish his spectacles.

The question about his guilt or innocence was repeated, but Edwards remained silent.

The clerk asked: "Did you hear what I said?"

Edwards still refused to speak. In order to break the deadlock, Edwards' solicitor, Mr. Lovibond, walked over to the dock and tried to reason with his obstinately mute client.

Eventually, Edwards was goaded into a reply of sorts. Adjusting his spectacles, he shouted: "I say you have no business to ask me such a question. It's stuff and nonsense."

In the absence of a reply to the question about his guilt or innocence, the judge directed that a plea of 'not guilty' should be entered.

Throughout the rest of the trial, Edwards displayed his contempt for the proceedings. During the prosecution's opening statement, Edwards shouted at Richard Muir, the prosecution counsel, "Now then young chappie, hurry up. I'm getting tired of it."

Given the overwhelming evidence that Edwards had killed, butchered and buried the Darby family, the only realistic option available to the defence was to argue that Edwards was insane. If the plea of insanity was accepted, Edwards could expect to be sent to the Criminal Lunatic Asylum (as it was then known) at Broadmoor. This appeared infinitely preferable to being hung, a fate which almost inevitably would follow without a successful plea of insanity.

Edwards' defence counsel, Percival Hughes, ingeniously tried to argue that the nature of the crime itself proved Edwards' insanity. "The enormity of the crime," he told the jury "and its conception and execution prove beyond all possible doubt that Edwards was suffering from a defect of reason. No sane man could have shown such a lust for blood. No novelist has achieved the heights of horror, nor had the genius to conceive a scheme of murder carried out on such a wholesale plan and for such trumpery motive as that which actuated the prisoner in the commission of this diabolical crime."

Other medical evidence was offered on both sides. In the end, the jury was unwilling to accept that Edwards was insane, and returned a verdict of guilty.

It had been expected that Edwards might respond to the verdict with a violent display of temper, and was surrounded by warders ready to restrain him. However, Edwards maintained his composure. When asked if he had anything to say as to why the death sentence should not be passed, Edwards responded in a hissing voice "No, get on with it. Get it over quickly."

As the judge put on the black cap — the traditional ritual before pronouncing a sentence of death — Edwards interrupted again, shouting: "This is like being on the stage. I wish, my lord, you would pass sentence on me as quickly as possible." When the judge had finished, Edwards gave out what one observer described as a harsh laugh. He then cast a final defiant look at the court, before being conducted to the cells below.

Edwards was executed on 3 March 1903.

The shop where the murders took place continued in business under new ownership. It also acquired a nickname: "The Little Shop of Horrors".

* * *

WAR AND PEACE

* * *

In March 1917, Percy Savage became the Divisional Detective Inspector (D.D.I.) in charge of the C.I.D. in 'F' Division of the Metropolitan Police. 'F' Division was new territory for Savage — it covered an area of west London, which included Paddington, Kensington and Notting Hill.

As D.D.I., Savage was in his element, because he saw a D.D.I. as "king of his own castle". As Savage explained:

"He is the officer held personally responsible by the Commissioner for the investigation of every crime committed in his division. There is no position that provides a police officer with a greater range of interesting work, or a better insight into lives of all types — the rich and the poor, the good and the evil, the weak and the strong, the cowards and the heroes."

However, a D.D.I. had to work long hours:

"My working day always started at nine o'clock in the morning, and it finished — well, I considered myself lucky if I got home at midnight.

In every case of serious crime the D.D.I. must personally conduct the investigation. It is absolutely essential that his subordinates know where he can be found at any hour of the day or night. If a murder is committed, he must at once inform the Assistant-Commissioner of the Criminal Investigation Department of the known facts and proceed with the inquiry without the loss of a minute.

The telephone was at my bedside, and it was not unusual for the divisional station or one of the sub-stations to ring me up during the night. Whether I was called up during the night or not, I made a point of being at my desk at nine o'clock sharp."

Whilst the D.D.I. in 'F' Division, Savage dealt with a murder by an Army officer who may have been suffering from 'shell shock'

* * *

3 The Tragedy of Two Army Doctors

* * *

13, Clarendon Road, Holland Park, London

13 January 1919

* * *

Late in the evening of 13 January 1919, Percy Savage was working in his room at Paddington Green police station when he received a telephone message that a man had been shot dead.

The dead man was an Army officer called Major Miles Seton. The case was unusual, because the identity of the killer was already known: another officer, Lieutenant Colonel Norman Rutherford, had been arrested for the murder and was in custody at Notting Hill police station.

It was nearly 11 p.m. when Savage received the message. He had looked forward to going home at about midnight, but that prospect now vanished completely. With Inspector Hanbrook and other officers, he drove to the scene of the killing, an impressive four storey house set back from the road in Holland Park.

13, Clarendon Road was the home of Sir Malcolm Seton, a distinguished civil servant. Major Seton, Sir Malcolm's cousin, was attached to the Australian Army Headquarters in London. The Seaton cousins got on well with each other, and Major Seaton was a regular visitor in Holland Park.

Percy Savage arrived at 13, Clarendon Road before midnight, and was joined by the pathologist, Sir Bernard Spilsbury.

Spilsbury found Major Seton's body lying in the hall of the house. He had been shot multiple times. Spilsbury counted fourteen wounds on the body. Some of the bullets had passed right through Seton's body following an almost horizontal path.

It was known that the first shots were fired in the dining room. In Spilsbury's opinion, Major Seton had been facing his killer across the dining table. When Rutherford drew his revolver, Seton started to walk backwards towards the door, but was shot twice in the chest before he could reach it. Then, as he tried to open the door, two more rounds hit him in the chest. Having opened the door, Seton moved towards the hall and turned, but collapsed before he got very far. He had also been wounded in the stomach and the arm.

* * *

In the early hours of 14 January, Percy Savage finished his inquiries at the house and went to Notting Hill police station. Savage found Lieutenant Colonel Rutherford "sitting in the detention room looking very depressed but, so far as I could judge, mentally calm."

"Are you in charge here?" Rutherford asked.

Savage replied that he was. Rutherford then made a request: "I should like to send a message to my wife telling her what has happened before it gets into the newspapers." Savage agreed to send any message that Rutherford wished to write, and gave him some paper and a pencil.

Rutherford wrote a message, but crumpled it up and threw it on the floor. Percy Savage retrieved the crumpled piece of paper, which read:

"Mrs. Rutherford, Carshalton Place, Carshalton, Surrey. The worst possible has happened. Seton is dead. — Norman."

Rutherford then wrote a second message, which he asked Savage to send to his wife. It read:

"I am sorry. An awful thing has happened. Seton is dead. — Norman."

* * *

Police were now able to piece together what happened on the night of the murder. Lieutenant Colonel Norman Rutherford, who was still serving in the Army, was on leave. He had been staying at Carshalton Place, Surrey, the family home which he shared with his wife, Alice, and their six children. During the evening of 13 January, he and Alice had a blazing argument.

After the row, Lieutenant Colonel Rutherford asked one of the maids at Carshalton Place to pack his bag. When the maid went upstairs and asked what he wanted packed, he replied rather strangely with the words "God knows, I don't." Then, seeing a revolver lying on the sofa, he added "You need not pack that as I shall not want it." When the bag was packed, he said "Don't lock it up. I have some cigars in the drawing room to put in."

Soon after 9 p.m., Rutherford caught the train at Carshalton Station for the short journey to London. Arriving at Victoria, he deposited his bag in the 'left luggage' part of the station cloakroom. Inside the bag was a bundle of five letters.

Rutherford then went to the District Messenger office (the office where telegrams were dispatched) and asked for a street directory, telling the clerk that he wanted to find Sir Malcolm Seton's address. Rutherford was highly anxious and unsettled, and was unable to find the address without help from the clerk. He noted the address down on paper, and called a taxi to take him to Clarendon Road.

Arriving at 13, Clarendon Road at 10.20 p.m, Rutherford rang the door bell. A maid answered the door and confirmed that this was Sir Malcolm Seton's house. Rutherford asked whether Major Seton was in.

He was in, but only as a result of a quirk of fate. That night, Major Seton had been due to sleep at the Australian Headquarters in Horseferry Road. However, when he reported for duty, he found that another officer was still using his room, so he went to his cousin's house in order to get a bed for the night.

Major Seton was upstairs in the smoking room, chatting with Sir Malcolm and Lady Seton. The maid went into the smoking room and announced that Lieutenant Colonel Rutherford was at the door.

Lady Seton assumed that Rutherford and Major Seton were friends, and asked the maid: "Won't you bring him up here?". However, Major Seton, perhaps sensing trouble replied, "Oh, I will just see what he wants", and went downstairs.

The two men went into the dining room and Major Seton pulled the door closed after them. About fifteen minutes later, Sir Malcolm and Lady Seton heard a number of pistol shots in very quick succession. Rushing downstairs, they found Major Seton, lying face-down in the hall. His feet were just inside the dining room, and his head was close to the foot of the stairs. Lieutenant Colonel Rutherford was still in the dining room, standing silent and motionless. His hands were down by his side, and his head was turned away from the body of Major Seton. In front of him, on the dining room table, lay his officer's cap, his gloves, his swagger stick (a small cane carried by officers) and a pistol.

"Did you do this?" asked Sir Malcolm.

"Yes," replied Lieutenant Colonel Rutherford. Sir Malcolm was struck by Rutherford's calmness. He spoke quietly, and without obvious emotion. However, when he saw Lady Seton, Rutherford gasped.

"You have killed Miles," said Lady Seton.

"Yes," Rutherford replied. "I only wish I had another bullet for myself."

Sir Malcolm and his wife tried to pick Major Seton up. However, the Major was a powerfully-built man, and difficult to move. Lady Seton remonstrated with Rutherford, asking him to help lift Major Seton, which he did.

The Major was still alive — just. He was groaning, and Lady Seton put the Major's head on her lap, trying to revive him with ammonia smelling salts rubbed on his lips. A few minutes later he died.

Lady Seton asked her husband to fetch a doctor. At first, Sir Malcolm hesitated, unsure whether it was wise to leave his wife alone in the house with a man who had just committed murder. In the end, however, he agreed to go, although not before extracting a promise from Lieutenant Colonel Rutherford that he would stay at the house.

After Sir Malcolm left, Rutherford became restless, and began pacing up and down the dining room, before moving to the dining table and picking up the pistol.

"Put that down at once," Lady Seton commanded. To her relief, Rutherford obeyed.

Lady Seton told Rutherford that he must promise not to touch the pistol again. He agreed, and let out a small laugh. "My dear lady," he said "I would not have given you that promise if it was of any use to me. It hasn't another bullet."

Lady Seton told Rutherford to bring the pistol to her. He complied immediately and handed it over. Lady Seton laid the pistol on the floor beside her.

Then, Rutherford took a letter out of his pocket, and asked Lady Seton "Will you do me a favour?" Lady Seton agreed, and Rutherford handed her a letter and asked her to burn it. She refused, but told the Lieutenant Colonel that, as she had promised to do him a favour, she would let him go upstairs and burn the letter on the fire in the smoking-room.

Rutherford did this, returning downstairs in time to hear the front door bell ring. Lady Seton asked him to open the front door. The caller was Miss Halse, the next door neighbour from 11, Clarendon Road. The drawing room of 11, Clarendon Road was immediately next door to the dining room of 13, Clarendon Road, and Miss Halse had been disturbed by the sound of shooting. Rather bravely, she had called to ask if anybody needed help.

Given that a murder had just taken place, an incongruous scene of stilted English politeness followed. Leaving Miss Halse at the door, Rutherford said he would talk to Lady Seton. Lady Seton, still sitting with Major Seton's body, told Rutherford that she would rather not see anybody. Rutherford returned to the front door, and gave Lady Seton's thanks and passed on the message that she was not receiving callers. Miss Hale returned next door, presumably somewhat confused.

Shortly afterwards, Dr. Browne, a local medical practitioner, arrived. He had been roused from his bed by Sir Malcolm Seton. Dr Browne examined Major Seton, and confirmed that he was dead. "A case of suicide, I suppose?" he asked, but was met by a shake of Lady Seton's head.

The next arrival was a uniformed officer from Notting Hill police station. In front of the officer, Sir Malcolm picked up the pistol, and asked Lieutenant Colonel Rutherford a direct question: "You admit you have murdered my cousin?"

"Yes," agreed Rutherford.

The constable arrested Rutherford, although giving him a chance to collect his officer's cap and gloves, before being taken to Notting Hill police station.

* * *

Why had Lieutenant Colonel Rutherford killed Major Seton? In the days following the murder, the police discovered more about the lives of the two men.

Major Miles Seton was 44 and unmarried. After studying medicine at Edinburgh University, he joined the Army as a Doctor, eventually transferring to the Australian Medical Corps. During the First World War, he served in Egypt, before working in various hospitals in England.

Lieutenant Colonel Norman Rutherford was 36. Like Miles Seton, he studied medicine at Edinburgh, before joining the Army as a Doctor. He had married his wife Alice against the wishes of Alice's father, who had higher social ambitions for his daughter. Shortly after the marriage, Alice followed her husband to South Africa: here, their first child was born in an Army tent. After returning from South Africa, the couple had five further children.

During the First World War, as a medical officer, Rutherford saw action at the sharp end. In 1917, he was nearly buried by shell-fire. For his actions treating the wounded under shell-fire he was awarded the Distinguished Service Order: the citation for the award referred to his "conspicuous gallantry".

The two men were old friends; Seton was godfather to Rutherford's youngest son. During the First World War, whilst Rutherford was serving on the Western Front, he told Seton, who was stationed in England, that he was welcome to spend time at the Rutherfords' family home, with Alice and the children.

This is where the trouble started. By the last year of the war, the Rutherfords' marriage was breaking down. Lieutenant Colonel Rutherford was prone to violent outbursts of temper. By the end of the war, Alice Rutherford had decided that she wanted a divorce. The couple failed to agree about who the three youngest children should live with: a bitter battle for custody of their children loomed.

With Miles Seton spending large amounts of time at the Rutherford family home, Alice Rutherford took to confiding in him about the state of her marriage. Although Lieutenant Colonel Rutherford claimed that he did not believe that Seton had an affair with Alice, he held Seton responsible for turning his wife and family against him.

The downward spiral of the Rutherfords' relationship could be traced through the letters which Lieutenant Colonel Rutherford had left in a bag at Victoria Station on the night of the murder. These had been written by Alice Rutherford, and set out the break-up of the marriage in painful detail. In one letter, Alice made it clear that she had had relationships with other men during their marriage.

The first of the letters was written in July, 1918. It suggested that, at this point, Alice held out hope that the marriage could be saved:

> "Your long letter came this evening, and the few words at the end rend my heart. Darling, have you ever known me merciless in refusing forgiveness? Only come back to me to help me to complete the task we undertook together. I believe my love for you to be the most vital part of me now, for in trying to put you out of my life, I have suffered tortures, both mental and physical . . . Love me with the strength of your being and I will not fail. Come back to me when the opportunity is given you, and I will be waiting as ever."

However, in a letter written in September 1918, it was clear that Alice Rutherford had given up hope. Divorce now seemed the only option:

> "You blamed me once for not being sufficiently candid with you, and this time I will be. I have been through hell this last week alone.
>
> I have not an atom of trust in your promise, and only away from you can I be happy again. This is my last word.
>
> I have struggled and tried, trusted and hoped, but the end is inevitable, and in common justice I had to tell you so. I shall take no steps, do nothing further, but only battle along alone as before.
>
> I am sorry for you, but I cannot act otherwise."

Two months later, another letter referred to the dispute over the custody of their children:

> "I want to gain my freedom with as little suffering as possible, and if for the children's sake you will agree to carry the thing

through with as little publicity as possible, I will hand you over the three elder children.

Honestly, I think that would be the happier for you. I should not feel you were utterly broken. Please make the rest of my task as easy as possible for the sake of all I have so far borne for you.

When I wrote to you about seven weeks ago explaining my real feelings with regard to my future, I knew you would in all probability attribute the cause of it to extreme mental and physical strain, due to what I was having to cope with quite alone at the time. I have, therefore, purposely waited for a reasonable time to elapse before writing to ask you to put no obstacle in the way of divorce if I bring an action against you."

This letter did not resolve the dispute over custody of the children. On 7 November 1918, in the closing days of the First World War, Alice Rutherford wrote to her husband:

"You intend to fight me for the children but you will never get them. You know well that through your awful temper and frequent ill-usage of me you have suffered greatly in the eyes of your children. Your love for me has been of the wrong kind; your love has always been artificial. The remainder of my life will be a curse to you evermore."

Then, on 29 November 1918, just over a fortnight after the Armistice, Alice Rutherford confirmed again her resolution to divorce:

"My Dear Norman.

The children were all delighted with their war souvenirs, which now adorn the library.

I am very unhappy. Candidly, other men have never been more than an episode in my life, but you were life itself. That does not alter the fact, I would give anything for a merciful providence to get me out of it. I do not think that anyone realises that love such as I can give you can never completely die nor be repeated. I am convinced that your nature can never change, and that only unhappiness lies with you."

* * *

Lieutenant Colonel Norman Rutherford's trial opened at the Old Bailey in April 1919.

As there was no doubt that Rutherford had killed Major Seton, the main issue in court was his state of mind when he pulled the trigger. His defence was conducted by a two man team, consisting of Travers Humphreys and Rigby Swift. Travers Humphreys was a barrister better known for prosecution work.

Humphreys and Swift considered possible lines of defence. One option was to try to explain Rutherford's actions in terms which would elicit sympathy. Rutherford was clearly a gallant soldier, with a distinguished war record. Whilst he had been fighting on the Western Front, he had been hospitable enough to throw open his home to his old friend and brother officer, Miles Seton. However, Seton had repaid him by turning his own wife and children against him.

However, Humphreys and Swift realised that there was a severe weakness with this approach. Rutherford had behaved badly towards his wife on a number of occasions, with violent outbursts of anger. It was hard to portray Rutherford simply as a victim.

Instead, Rutherford's defence team decided to examine his medical records and service history to see if they offered any scope for a defence. Rutherford's medical history showed that he had suffered concussion after a blow to the head during a football game in France in 1917. He also suffered badly from eczema, which flared up at particularly stressful times. During his service on the Western Front, Rutherford's eczema had caused insomnia, as well as affecting his mood. Officers and men who had served with him reported that when Rutherford's eczema was at its worst, he was prone to savage tempers, sometimes of a ferocity which frightened his subordinates.

Rutherford's service records also showed that he had nearly been buried by shell-fire. This had caused some noticeable behavioural changes — he was described as "behaving oddly" after this incident. During the First World War, the British Army had begun to recognise the condition of 'shell-shock', although it was still poorly understood. It is feasible that the trauma of war had affected Rutherford's mind.

Humphreys and Rigby decided that the best course of action for Rutherford was to plead insanity. At the trial, a number of witnesses were called to give a fuller idea of Rutherford's character and mental state. Lieutenant Colonel Francis Hill from the Royal Army Medical Corps told the court that Rutherford's war record had been a distinguished one: Rutherford had acted with courage doing his duty at the front. Other soldiers who had served alongside Rutherford testified about his wildly fluctuating moods, and his frightening outbursts of temper.

One piece of medical evidence was particularly compelling. A doctor explained that whilst serving in France in 1918, Lieutenant Colonel Rutherford had:

"a vivid dream in which he went through the full horror of having killed Major Seton, and that he wakened in a condition of terror. He viewed the whole dream with horror and put it away from him. Subsequently the idea would recur from time to time, until it assumed in his mind the form of a definite premonition.

I asked him why he fired so many shots at Major Seton, and he replied 'Because I dislike to see anything wounded.' He also said he would do the same again. I am of the definite opinion that at the time of the commission of the act he did not know the difference between right and wrong, and at the time, and right up to now, he honestly believed he was doing right."

It was part of the defence team's strategy to insist that Lieutenant Colonel Rutherford did not believe that Miles Seton was having an affair with Alice Rutherford. They wanted to avoid the implication that Lieutenant Colonel Rutherford had a genuine basis for holding a grudge against Miles Seton, in case the prosecution used this to support the idea that Rutherford fully understood what he was doing on the night of the murder. Instead, the defence insisted that Rutherford was simply in the grip of an irrational belief that Seton had turned his wife and children against him.

Other evidence was given about Rutherford's state of mind at the time of the crime. The maid who let Rutherford into Sir Malcolm Seton's house told the court that:

"He struck me as being like a man who has been dozing and is waking up."

The jury was told that, after the crime, Rutherford had been calm, and had made no attempt to cover up the crime, or to escape. It was as if, having committed murder, Rutherford's sense of fury and outrage had left him. After the attack, he seemed relatively tranquil, and between the murder and the trial, had slept well and had gained weight.

Another specialist, Dr. Francis Henry Edwards, gave his opinion that Rutherford had been incapable of appreciating the difference between right and wrong on the night of the murder.

In his summing up at Rutherford's trial, Mr. Justice Salter said it was of the gravest importance that juries should not accept the suggestion of insanity lightly: instead, they must see that it was fully proved to their complete satisfaction, otherwise human life might be in grave danger.

It took the jury only five minutes to come back with their verdict: Rutherford was insane. Mr. Justice Salter said he agreed with the verdict, and Rutherford was sent to the Criminal Lunatic Asylum at Broadmoor.

* * *

Major Miles Seton was buried with full military honours at Brookwood Military Cemetery, Surrey. His coffin was covered with the Union Jack, and a firing party of Australian troops led the procession.

Rutherford spent the next 10 years at Broadmoor. Broadmoor is next door to Wellington College, the public school, and a regular cricket fixture was played between Wellington staff and Broadmoor staff and patients.

At one of these cricket matches, Rutherford met Hugh Scott, a master at Wellington College. After their meeting, Scott and another school master, Gordon Carey, took to visiting Rutherford at Broadmoor.

Scott and Carey were struck by Rutherford's intelligence, and by his writing ability. The three men agreed to work together to produce a history of the First World War. Rutherford was to be the main author, with a small number of chapters contributed by Scott, and Carey acting as overall editor.

The result was *An Outline History of the Great War*, published in 1928. However, Home Office regulations prevented Rutherford being named as the author. The book was published under the names of Scott and Carey, with an acknowledgement in the preface that the book could not have been written without the contributions of an 'anonymous friend'.

Scott sent a copy of the book to the Home Secretary, explaining the part which Rutherford had played in writing it. Shortly afterwards, the Home Secretary decided that Rutherford could be released from Broadmoor.

After release, Rutherford lived abroad in Canada, Austria and then in the Middle East: it appears that leaving England was either a condition of Rutherford's release, or at least was thought by him to be a wise course of action. In 1950, he returned briefly to Yorkshire, the county of his birth, before going to South Africa where he died in 1951. Lieutenant Colonel Rutherford requested that he should be buried with his old Army steel helmet — the one which he had worn as a medical officer on the Western Front.

Alice Rutherford continued to try to divorce her husband. Surprising as it seems today, the restrictive nature of divorce law at the time meant that, despite Rutherford's conviction for murder, there were still significant obstacles to getting a divorce. In 1928, Alice changed her name, reverting to her maiden name of 'Roberts'. Eventually, a divorce was granted in 1938 on the grounds of cruelty, allowing her to re-marry.

Alice — now Alice Clark — lived until 1982, dying on the Isle of Man at the age of 100.

SURPRISING VIOLENCE

* * *

The next two chapters deal with murders in which a killing resulted from what seems to have been a surprising over-reaction.

'The Hunt for the Police Killers' deals with the brutal murder of a police officer in 1927. The killers were car thieves who were stopped by an unarmed police officer on foot patrol: instead of simply driving off, the car thieves stopped and shot the police officer four times. Percy Savage became involved in one aspect of this case after being promoted to Detective Chief Superintendent, in charge of the Central Office of the C.I.D. at Scotland Yard.

'Murder by Moonlight' deals with a murder in 1931, in which the killers were seeking revenge against a man who had stolen a small quantity of food from them. The case is interesting because it gives an insight into a lost world — the world of a shanty town on the edge of north London, where a small community of men lived in makeshift huts and shelters hidden in the woods.

* * *

4 The Hunt for the Police Killers

* * *

Stapleford Abbotts, Essex

September 1927

* * *

Shortly before 6 a.m. on 27 September 1927, P.C. George Gutteridge was found dead by the side of the road at Stapleford Abbotts, half way between Romford and Ongar.

His body, which was in a pool of blood, was propped against a grass bank. He was in a half-sitting, half-lying position, with his legs sticking out towards the middle of the road. Both of his eyes had been shot out, and he had two further bullet wounds on his left cheek. He was clutching a pencil in his right hand, as if he had been shot whilst about to write in his notebook; his notebook and helmet were lying on the ground nearby, and his whistle was hanging from his pocket.

It appeared that George Gutteridge had been dead for a while. William Ward, a local resident was the first person to find him dead: when he took hold of Gutteridge's right hand, it was cold.

There was a large splash of blood in the centre of the road, as well as more splashes of blood leading across to the body. The trail of blood suggested that George Gutteridge had been in the centre of the road when he was shot. He had then staggered back to the bank where he now lay. A tyre mark from a car could be seen close to the bank on the opposite side of the road.

It was soon established that the last person to report seeing George Gutteridge alive was another police officer, P.C. Sydney Taylor. Both officers had been on duty on the Romford-Ongar

Road overnight. At 3 a.m., Gutteridge and Taylor met near Grove House, Howe Green, a police 'conference point' (in the era before officers were equipped with personal radios, officers on the beat met at pre-arranged times at 'conference points'). Sydney Taylor then walked to his home in nearby Lambourne End. Gutteridge also started to walk home, to Townley Cottages in Stapleford Abbotts, where he lived with Rose, his wife, and their two children, Muriel and Jack.

Townley Cottages was about a mile away from the police conference point: Gutteridge only managed to walk 600 yards before being shot.

On being informed about the discovery of P.C. Gutteridge, the Chief Constable of Essex, Captain Unett, decided to call in Scotland Yard. This made perfect sense: Stapleford Abbotts was close to the boundary of the area covered by the Metropolitan Police, and it seemed possible that the murderers had come from London or had some connection with it. At Scotland Yard, Chief Inspector James Berrett, assisted by Detective Sergeant Harris, was assigned to the case.

The first step in the investigation was a thorough examination of the murder scene. Measurements and photographs were taken. In addition to the tyre mark by the roadside bank, there was a scratch on a stone, possibly caused by a car. No other tyre marks could be found on the road surface.

Two bullets were found at the scene. One of the bullets which had gone through Gutteridge's eyes was lodged in the ground. Another bullet, which had passed through Gutteridge's cheek, fell out of his uniform when his body was moved. Gutteridge's body was later taken to the Royal Oak in Stapleford Abbotts, where it was placed in a cart-lodge overnight. He was moved to the Romford mortuary on the morning of Wednesday 28 September.

* * *

The first break-through in the investigation came less than 24 hours after the murder.

On the night of 26 September, a car belonging to a medical practitioner, Dr. Lovell, had been stolen from Billericay, twelve miles away from the murder scene. This led officers to wonder whether the car thief (or thieves) had used the quiet back roads near Stapleford Abbotts to drive the car back to London under cover of darkness. Very little traffic passed along the Romford-Ongar road at night, and it was possible that P.C. Gutteridge had challenged the car to stop, leading to him being shot. Counting against this theory, however, was the fact that it seemed unlikely that car thieves would go about their business armed, or would try to shoot their way out when challenged by a police officer on foot.

A description of the stolen car was circulated to police stations in Essex and the Metropolitan area. On 27 September, the police received a report that a car had been abandoned in an alley behind Foxley Road, Brixton. This proved to be the car which had been stolen from Billericay the night before.

The car was towed back to Brixton police station for further inspection. During the search of the car, a spent cartridge from a military revolver was found on the floor under one of the seats. Soil samples and dried grass were taken from the near-side tyres. Minor dents in the car were noted, and impressions of finger-prints were taken from the steering wheel.

There were dark spots on the car's off-side running board: the running board was detached and sent to the Home Office laboratory in Chancery Lane. The Home Office chemist reported that the spots were bloodstains (today, the running board is an exhibit in Scotland Yard's Museum of objects associated with notorious crimes). The soil samples were similar to the soil found at the roadside in Stapleford Abbotts — although, on its own, this was not enough evidence to positively link the car to the murder scene. The dried grass on the car's tyres showed that the car had gone over a grassed area, similar to the grass bank by the

Romford-Ongar road. The dents on the car suggested that it had run into something.

Excitement increased on 29 September, when a boy found a revolver by the River Thames at Hammersmith; on 30 September, a tin box containing cartridges was found abandoned on some waste ground nearby. However, examination by a ballistics expert showed that the revolver could not have fired the bullets found at Stapleford Abbotts. It was also found that the tin box had been lying on the waste ground for some time, and had not been abandoned after the murder.

Another false start occurred on the evening of 29 September. Hampshire police telephoned the investigating team, who were working out of the police station at Romford, with the news that a man had confessed to the murder. The man was in custody in Basingstoke.

Officers set off on an overnight journey from Essex to Hampshire, a trip made difficult by thick fog. The man was interviewed in Basingstoke at 5 a.m., and then taken back to Romford. However, the man's confession quickly unravelled, and he was released. He turned out to be an attention-seeker, who had made a bogus confession a few years before, in a different murder case.

The focus of the enquiry was now on finding who had been in the stolen car. House-to-house enquiries were made in Brixton, but this did not produce any information. Although detectives thought that they were looking for somebody from London, the possibility had to be considered that the murderer was somebody local to Stapleford Abbotts.

In what was still a fairly rural district of Essex, gossip flowed freely, and many locals reported their suspicions to police. The name of one man, who was alleged to own firearms, came up a number of times. Chief Inspector Berrett thought that this man was essentially an eccentric, rather than a potential murderer. Nevertheless, Berrett felt compelled to interview him. After an interview, which took place in a local barn and lasted three and a half hours, the man was eliminated from the enquiry.

Another local man was reported to the police as having boasted about being connected to the murder. This man had previous convictions but, in fact, had nothing to do with the killing of P.C. Gutteridge. However, when he was interviewed, police discovered that he was still wanted for a completely different offence, for which he was duly prosecuted and sentenced.

The circumstances of P.C. Gutteridge's life also had to be investigated, in order to find out if somebody might have a grudge against him. Gutteridge's neighbours in Stapleford Abbotts were questioned. It transpired that Gutteridge was a happily married man with a steady temperament, who appeared to have no obvious enemies.

The investigating team spent many hours trawling through criminal records, looking for criminals who were known to carry firearms, and might be willing to use them against the police. One man whose record attracted attention had recently been released from prison after serving a 15 year sentence for the manslaughter of a police officer. After his release he had committed an offence in Billericay. Police visited the address which the man had given police on his release, and found a bloodstained bandage and a collection of newspaper reports of Gutteridge's murder. However, the man himself had disappeared.

As a result, his photograph was published in the Police Gazette and in daily newspapers. When the man presented himself at Scotland Yard, he protested that he had been at a night club on the night of the murder. This story was confirmed by inspection of the club register and by witnesses who had been at the club at the relevant time, so the man was allowed to go free.

As officers went through criminal records, one other name stood out early in the investigation — Frederick Guy Browne, sometimes known as 'Leo' Browne.

Detective Superintendent Savage knew Browne very well. Some years earlier, one of Savage's officers, Inspector Lawrence, had arrested Browne at Southend in connection with a series of motor insurance frauds: Browne had told officers that he would never be captured alive again, and that he would shoot the next police officer who tried to arrest him. Browne was generally known as a 'hard case', who appeared to have a grudge against the police.

Other factors made Browne a suspect. He worked in the motor-trade, and had a history of motor crime, which started during the First World War, when he deserted from the Army after stealing a motorbike. At the time of the Gutteridge murder, Browne had only just come out of prison after serving a sentence for car theft. Crucially, Browne knew the area in which Gutteridge was murdered, having worked in a garage in Essex. However, police did not know where Browne was, and had no way of questioning him.

* * *

Despite extensive enquiries, by the time that the inquest into P.C. Gutteridge's death was concluded in November 1927, there was a sense that the investigation had reached a standstill. However, in that month, a seemingly trivial incident took place which was to change the course of the investigation.

A man called Mr. Mincher was driving his van in Sheffield. The van was going through a narrow railway arch, when a car approached at speed from the other direction. Mr. Mincher swerved to avoid hitting the car; the van collided with the railway arch, scraping its wing. The driver of the car refused to give Mr. Mincher his name or address, and drove off.

Mr. Mincher noted down the car's number plate 'XK2508', and reported the accident to P.C. James Ward of Sheffield police. Shortly afterwards, P.C. Ward saw the car, stopped it, and took the driver's details. These were shown on the driver's licence as Sydney Rhodes of 27, York Terrace, Clapham Road, Stockwell. P.C. Ward also noted that there was a passenger in the car.

Sheffield police issued a summons against Rhodes for reckless driving. However, when an attempt was made to serve the summons on the address in Stockwell, it was discovered that the name and address on the licence were false — the licence was a fake. It was also discovered that the car's number plate was a fake copy: the registration 'XK2508' properly belonged to a London taxi.

Shortly afterwards, in Sheffield, P.C. Ward saw the man who had been a passenger in the car when Ward stopped it to take the driver's details. Ward detained the man, and took him in for questioning.

The man told police that the driver of the car was called Frederick Browne, and that he had been in Sheffield to sell a car which he had stolen in Tooting. He added that Browne ran a garage in Northcote Road, Battersea. The man had a criminal past, and had met Browne when they were both in Dartmoor, but it seemed as if he now wanted to distance himself from Browne, perhaps regarding Browne as 'too hot to handle'.

Further information came to the police at the end of December, when Scotland Yard received a letter from Sheffield. In the letter, the writer said that he was in a position to give the police information about recent armed robberies at railway stations. He added that if the police got the two men involved in these robberies, it was "a thousand to one" that they would also have caught the murderer of P.C. Gutteridge.

Scotland Yard asked Sheffield police for more information about the writer of the letter: it turned out to be the passenger in Browne's car who had already been questioned by Sheffield police. The *News of the World* had offered a £2,000 reward (approximately £120,000 in today's money) for any information leading to the arrest of P.C. Gutteridge's killer: the man later received the £2,000 reward.

* * *

Now that Scotland Yard had information that Browne had stolen a car, and that he ran a garage in Battersea, Chief Inspector Berrett decided that he should be arrested. His garage at 7, Northcote Road was kept under watch. Towards the end of January 1928, Browne left London for a few days and, whilst he was away, a number of officers concealed themselves in the office of the garage.

Browne returned to London on 20 January. He drove his car — the stolen car which had been involved in the accident in Sheffield — into the garage yard at 7.30 p.m. As he went into his office, he was seized immediately, and tightly guarded.

Browne, the car and the garage were searched thoroughly. In the driver's side pocket of the car there was a fully loaded Webley revolver, and in a secret compartment behind the driver's seat there was another military revolver. There was also a pair of forceps and a jemmy in the car.

12 cartridges were found in Browne's pockets. He was carrying a mask, with cut-out holes for his eyes and nose, and a forged driving licence in the name of Harris. In the garage, the police found 16 cartridges, another pair of forceps, a tube of ethyl-chloride, bandages, a scalpel case and boric lint. Browne's home at 33, Sisters Avenue, Battersea was also searched, and here police found a fully loaded revolver, a number of cartridges and an ear speculum.

On being searched Browne said "That's done it. Now you've found them it's all up with me". Browne also told police officers "If you had stopped me while I was in the car, I should have shot five of you and kept the other for myself. From what I can see of it, I should have to make a machine gun for you boys next time."

Browne was taken to Tooting police station, and charged with the theft of the car. It has to be remembered that, at this stage, Scotland Yard had no direct evidence linking Browne to the Gutteridge murder. Scotland Yard now wanted to find the link.

Inspector Betteridge travelled from Scotland Yard to Tooting to ask Browne to account for his movements on the night of 26 September 1927. Browne told detectives that, on the night of Gutteridge's murder he was with his wife at home in Sisters Avenue, Battersea. In his statement, he denied any knowledge of the murder:

"I have heard of Stapleford Abbotts, but don't remember ever having been through it. I think the first time I heard about the murder was when a policeman came to my garage and passed some remark. I do not take newspapers in, because I do not read them. I have not the patience. My wife has a picture paper each day, and I think she passed some remark about it.

I have been asked by Chief Inspector Berrett to account for the Webley revolver found in my possession, which was loaded in six chambers. I wish to say I have never fired the revolver since I first had it.

I got it some time in April last. I gave £3 for it down at Tilbury Docks from a sailorman whose name I do not know, neither can I describe him. The ammunition with which it is loaded I obtained from another man, together with a number of other cartridges shown to me, which were found in my hip-pocket.

I knew the man I got the ammunition from in the Army. I do not wish to say who the man is. The ammunition is very old type. Shortly after I got the revolver it began to go rusty, but I kept it well oiled. I have never used it.

I loaded it so that it would frighten any one in case they interfered, and the reason I carried the weapon was because at the beginning of the war, when I was working for Pytchley Auto Car Company, Great Portland Street, delivering cars by road, once when I was going through Gloucester to South Wales, a man at dusk signalled to me when I was driving the car to stop . . . and as I was engaged on the near side speaking to him, two other men jumped on the off-side running board and demanded money.

I was unprepared, and gave them what little money I had. Some six weeks after that occasion, when going to Bournemouth with another car, the same kind of thing happened to me with a man calling on me to stop, but I declined. After this I made up my mind to be armed when taking cars to the country, and I purchased a revolver with a long barrel, but I had no ammunition.

I later joined the Army, but have never been threatened since. The reason I had it on me today was because I had been on a country run to Devon.

I have never been out in Essex at night driving motor cars or taking part in stealing motor cars."

In his statement, Browne explained the various medical items found in his possession by saying that lint, bandages and ethyl-chloride were kept in the garage as part of a first aid kit. It was unclear, of course, how this explanation accounted for the pairs of forceps and the ear speculum found during the search.

* * *

After Browne gave his statement, Chief Inspector Berrett went to Sheffield to interview the man who had been a passenger in the stolen car, and had written a letter to Scotland Yard. The man confirmed that he had associated extensively with Browne, as well as with a garage assistant called 'Pat', who worked for Browne.

The man was convinced from what Browne and 'Pat' had said in conversation that the pair were involved in the Gutteridge murder. Using photographs held in the Criminal Record Office, the man was able to identify 'Pat' as William Henry Kennedy, an ex-convict sometimes known by the nickname 'Ginger'.

Officers now wanted to bring Kennedy in for questioning. On 21 January, the day after Browne's arrest, Kennedy went to the garage, but found it locked. He also saw some men who he thought were detectives.

Kennedy had only been married three days earlier. Worried that police were at the garage, Kennedy, accompanied by his wife, left London in a hurry. Police found that the couple had gone to Liverpool. As Superintendent of the Central Office of the C.I.D., Percy Savage was responsible for overseeing officers sent outside London: in order to trail Kennedy, he sent two officers, Inspector Kirchner and Sergeant Duncan.

It was likely that Kennedy was armed, so Savage told Kirchner and Duncan that he was willing to issue them with revolvers. However, they refused. During his time as a Superintendent, Savage only issued revolvers to officers on two occasions. This was the era when the culture of British policing was very much against arming officers, if it could be avoided. Savage argued that:

"To equip them with revolvers or pistols would tend to destroy the whole tone and value of their work. If the police were armed, an ever-increasing number of criminals would also arm themselves, and it would follow that householders and shopkeepers would think it necessary that they should carry loaded guns and pistols to protect themselves against the growing hordes of dangerous criminals. I do not wish to comment upon conditions in the United States — they have troubles peculiarly their own — but it is obvious that if the police of England were armed with automatics, criminals would reply with machine guns, and so the vicious circle would continue until every citizen was armed, and every home an arsenal."

In Liverpool, Kennedy and his wife took lodgings in Copperas Hill, under the name of O'Donnell. Liverpool police found out where Kennedy was, and officers from London and Liverpool took positions around the lodgings to keep watch.

At 11.45 p.m. on 25 January Kennedy left the lodgings. He was clearly worried that he was being watched — he had pulled the brim of his hat down and turned the collar of his coat up. He was also trying to cover his face with his left hand, and was walking briskly.

As he walked away, he was challenged by Detective Sergeant Mattinson from Liverpool police. Mattinson knew Kennedy well, and shouted: "Now then, come on Bill."

Kennedy spun round, and drew a pistol from his pocket, shouting at Mattinson "Stand back, or I'll shoot". He then pushed the barrel of the pistol into Mattinson's chest, and pulled the trigger.

The pistol was fully loaded. However, Kennedy had forgotten to release the safety catch. As he pulled the trigger, the weapon clicked, but it didn't fire. Seizing his opportunity, Mattinson grabbed Kennedy's arm, and wrenched the pistol off him.

According to Mattinson:

"I immediately closed with him. I gripped Kennedy's right hand, holding the revolver with my left hand, and twisted his arm in doing it. At the same time I struck him a blow on the right side of his face and neck. This partially knocked him off his balance, turning his back to me. I then grabbed him by the back of the coat collar with my right hand and thrust the point of the revolver into his left side and began pushing him back. I was met by Inspector Kirschner and another officer. As they reached me I held the revolver up in my left hand and shouted: 'It's all right. I have got it.' I went sick and partially collapsed, but recovered."

Other officers rushed up and held Kennedy, who later told Mattinson "You ought to be in heaven by this time." Mattinson was awarded the King's Police Medal for his part in Kennedy's arrest.

* * *

Kennedy was taken to Scotland Yard, travelling by train. With police permission, Kennedy's wife travelled in the same compartment with him.

At Scotland Yard, Chief Inspector Berrett asked Kennedy if he knew anything about the murder of P.C. Gutteridge. Kennedy replied "I may be able to tell you something, but let me think a while."

Kennedy then said that he wanted to see his wife. She was brought into the room, and he told her: "After I was arrested at Liverpool, I told you there was something more serious at the back of it. Well, there is. These officers are making inquiries about the policeman who was murdered in Essex."

"You didn't murder him?" his wife asked.

"No, I did not, but I was there, and I know who did. If I am charged with the murder and found guilty, I shall be hanged, and you will be a widow. On the other hand, if I am charged and found guilty of being an accessory after the fact, I shall receive a severe sentence and be a long time from you. Will you wait for me?"

"Yes, love, I will wait for you" she replied. "Tell the gentlemen the truth of what took place."

"All right, I will. Take down what I say and I will sign it."

Kennedy made a statement, in which he admitted his involvement on the night of the murder, but tried to put the blame for the killing on Browne. In the statement, Kennedy described how he and Browne had stolen the doctor's car in Billericay:

"The time was then, I should think, about 11 p.m.. We walked through the village again and came to a spot, which

I now know is the doctor's house, on a sharp bend . . . on the main London road.

We saw the garage at the end of the doctor's house, and we went into the field opposite, and sat on some old palings or gates, and waited till the lights went out in the doctor's house. It was getting late and must have been after midnight. After the lights went out, Browne and I went to the garage, which is a wooden structure, and he forced the doors with, I think, a small tyre lever or tool of some kind, which he took with him. The door opened easily.

He first examined the petrol tank and make of car. He told me it was a Morris-Cowley. It ran down on its own weight to the road, and we pushed it along abound a hundred yards in the opposite direction, or at a right angle to the main road.

Browne said 'We will go by the byways and escape the main road'. We then went for a long run round country lanes at a great pace at different times. We got to several cross-roads and corners, where it was necessary for us to examine the sign posts, but eventually we got on to a kind of main road on the way to Ongar.

When we got some distance up this road we saw someone who stood on the bank and flashed his lamp as a signal to stop. We drove on, and then I heard a police whistle, and told Browne to stop. He did so quite willingly, and when the person came up we saw it was a policeman.

Browne was driving, and I was sitting on his left in the front. The policeman came up close to the car and stood near Browne, and asked where he was going and where he came from. Browne told him we came from Lea Bridge Road garage, and had been out to do some repairs.

The policeman then asked if he had a card. Browne said 'No'. He then asked Browne 'Do you have a driving licence?' Browne again said 'No'. The policeman again asked him where he came from, and Browne stammered in his answer, and the policeman then said 'Is the car yours?' I then said 'No, the car is mine.'

The policeman flashed his light in both our faces, and at this time was standing close to the running board on the off-side. He then asked me if I knew the number of the car, and Browne said 'You'll see it on the front of the car'.

The policeman said 'I know the number, but do you?' I said 'Yes, I can give you the number,' and said TW 6120.' He said 'Very well, I'll take particulars,' put his torch back in his pocket, and pulled out his notebook, and was in the act of writing when I heard a report, quickly followed by another one.

I saw the policeman stagger back and fall over by the bank at the hedge. I said to Browne 'What have you done?' and then saw he had a large Webley revolver in his hand. He said 'Get out quick.' I immediately got out and went round to the policeman, who was lying on his back, and Browne came over and said 'I'll finish the bugger' and I said 'For God's sake, don't shoot any more, the man's dying,' as he was groaning.

The policeman's eyes were open, and Browne, addressing him, said 'What are you looking at me like that for?' and, stooping down, shot him at close range through both eyes. There were only four shots fired.

Browne then said 'Let's get back into the car.' We had driven close into the bank, and backed out a little, and drove in the direction of Ongar. He gave me the revolver, and told me to load it while he drove on. I loaded it, and in my excitement I dropped an empty shell in the car. The other three I threw away into the roads.

We drove at great pace through many villages, the names of which I do not know, but I do know that we went through Buckhurst Hill, and then Bow and Elephant and Castle, and while on this journey Browne said 'Have you loaded that gun again? If you have, give it me back.' I gave it to him, and he kept it on the seat by his right-hand side.

He wanted to take the car to the garage, but I persuaded him to have nothing to do with the garage. We drove to Brixton and drove into a cul-de-sac at about 5.30 a.m.. We left the car and came out of the main road, and came by tramcar back to the garage, bringing with us two cases out of the car containing doctor's instruments. These, or the majority of them, were smashed up, and the cases were cut up into small pieces, which Browne later took out in his car and distributed about various roads in the country, so as to destroy all evidence.

I forgot to mention that on our journey, Browne turned into a tree owing to fog at a gate. The fog was very dense at the time. I think he damaged the near-side front wing. I was very excited at the time. We returned to the garage at 6 a.m., and commenced our work.

I then suggested that we should go right away from London, as I knew enquiries were sure to be made. Browne said there was no danger, and induced me to stop, and said that if I made up my mind to leave him, he would blow my brains out. He had the Webley revolver in his hand when he said this and, as I knew that it was loaded, I thought he would.

I then later went to a newspaper shop and purchased the various editions of the papers, and in one I found that Scotland Yard was supposed to have found finger-prints, and again wanted to leave, and he said 'No you don't; you'll stop here and face it out with me. If anybody comes here there will be a shooting match.'

I remained in the garage till December, and we saw newspapers on different dates relating to the crime, and saw the renewed inquest in November, and the reward in the *News of the World*, and Browne said 'They're still harping on that thing yet.' "

* * *

At Scotland Yard, Percy Savage received the news that Kennedy had made a statement. He wrote:

> "During the time I was Superintendent of the Central Office at New Scotland Yard, there were many occasions when I felt proud of the really brilliant work done by officers of the Criminal Investigation Department, but perhaps the proudest moment of all was when, sitting in my room in New Scotland Yard, I received the news that Frederick Guy Browne had been unmasked as one of the two men who had murdered Police Constable Gutteridge."

Later, Savage was dragged into a dispute about whether Kennedy's statement had been obtained under duress. Kennedy made the statement at about 8 p.m., having spent most of the day travelling from Liverpool. According to Kennedy, he had not been given enough rest or food during the day, and ended up "in a state of mental helplessness" where he "did not know what he was doing or signing". Kennedy thought that the statement had been "pumped out" of him "by four hours of interrogation, of promises, hopes, and threats." Percy Savage, as Superintendent of the Central Office of the C.I.D., had overall responsibility for Kennedy's treatment whilst in Scotland Yard's custody. According to Savage "Kennedy suggested that I was the evil genius who had by some subtle art played upon his delicate feelings to such an extent that he was persuaded against his better judgment to make his confession."

In truth, it seems likely that Kennedy did face "promises, hopes and threats" to induce him to write his statement. Clearly, Kennedy believed that, by implicating Browne for the murder, he could avoid being charged with the crime himself. Kennedy's statement shows that he thought that he would only be charged as an "accessory after the fact" — in other words as somebody who had assisted a murderer, but not actually committed a murder. It seems feasible to imagine that the Scotland Yard team misled Kennedy into believing this: in other words, Kennedy was told "tell us what happened, and you'll get off more lightly."

In fact, the opposite applied — by admitting to having been in the stolen car at the murder scene, Kennedy laid himself open to being charged with the murder. This was on the grounds that he had been part of a "joint enterprise" with Browne. Under the principle of "joint enterprise", it did not matter who had actually pulled the trigger. Kennedy was a simple man, who could not be expected to have an understanding of the criminal law. If police had not misled him into thinking that he was protecting himself by making a statement, it is hard to see why he was willing to do so.

One other point in Kennedy's statement can be commented on. Shooting P.C. George Gutteridge through the eyes whilst he lay on the roadside may seem pointless and brutal. However, although undoubtedly brutal, this action may have had a particular motive. There was a widespread folklore belief that a dead person's eyes acted as a 'tell-tale': in other words, at the point of death, a person's eyes recorded a photographic impression of their last sight. It is quite possible that this belief led to P.C. Gutteridge's eyes being shot out.

* * *

Browne and Kennedy were charged with murder on Monday 6 February 1928.

Although Kennedy's statement could be used to incriminate him, the law dictated that it would not be admissible in evidence against Browne. In order to make a case against Browne, police turned to ballistics evidence. Robert Churchill, a gun maker, examined the empty cartridge which had been left on the floor of the car stolen from Billericay. He also examined the Webley revolver found in the pocket of Browne's car on the day of his arrest. The cartridge was of the 'Mark IV' pattern, a type which had last been used by the British Army in 1914. Two of the bullets which killed P.C. Gutteridge were of the same calibre, as was the Webley revolver.

Churchill examined the cartridge and Browne's revolver under a microscope, and was able to show that the cartridge had been fired from the revolver. Churchill's conclusion depended on the idea that the revolver had its own "gun print" — in other words, its own unique characteristics, acquired in the course of its manufacture, which distinguished it from any other weapon.

The breech shield of Browne's revolver had been filed by hand, leaving a unique set of marks. When the revolver was fired, these marks were transferred to the cartridge (because the recoil of the revolver pushed the cartridge against the breech shield, leaving an impression on the cartridge). Enlarged photographs of the breech shield and the cartridge allowed for the correspondence between the two sets of marks to be checked. Ballistics experts at the War Office were called on to confirm Churchill's findings.

No finger-prints were found in the car, and it seems that both Browne and Kennedy were careful to wear gloves on the day of the murder. Given this caution, it seems surprising that Browne kept the revolver which had been used to kill P.C. Gutteridge. If he had thrown the revolver away, it seems likely that the police would not have been able to pursue a case against him.

* * *

Browne and Kennedy's trial opened on 23 April 1928. The trial judge was Mr. Justice Avory, the same judge who had presided over the Mahon trial — already discussed in Chapter One — four years earlier.

The prosecution case was that the principle of 'joint enterprise' meant that it did not matter who had shot P.C. Gutteridge, provided that the jury was satisfied that at least one of the men had pulled the trigger:

"The case for the Crown is that Police Constable Gutteridge was shot by one or both of these men, and that, even if it is left uncertain whether the actual shooting was done by one or by both of them, if you are satisfied that both, being jointly engaged in stealing that Morris-Cowley car, were united in the common resolution to resist by violence anyone who should oppose them, and if the murder were committed in pursuance of that common resolution, both the prisoners were guilty, although one only may have fired the shots."

Giving evidence, Browne stuck by his story that he had never fired any of the revolvers, and that it was pure fabrication to hold that he had been in Stapleford Abbotts on the night of the murder. For his part, Kennedy explained that he had not told the police about the murder until January 1928 because he was terrified. He also continued to disassociate himself from Browne:

"I thought that if it were known that I was present at the time of the murder I should have been accused of it, although I was completely innocent. I can only express my deep regret to Mrs. Gutteridge that I was in the car at the time of the murder."

When the jury returned with their verdict, the dock was heavily guarded, because of a fear that Browne might make a revenge attack on Kennedy. The jury found both Browne and Kennedy guilty but, in the event, both men remained calm and impassive — they "heard their fate without moving an eyelash" as Percy Savage put it.

The way in which Browne and Kennedy reacted when found guilty was somewhat at odds with their reputation as violent desperadoes. Both men were asked if they had anything to say why a sentence of death should not be passed. Browne smiled and said:

> "I will admit that the counsel have acted very fairly as far as I am concerned. I admit that I would not wish to be tried by a better judge, but the jury have had stuff given to them which is not genuine. It will come out later that I had nothing to do with it, but I am not going to argue the point. I am quite content. My conscience is clear."

Kennedy, speaking softly, said:

> "I am not afraid of death. I shall die willingly, because I have a certain knowledge that in the hereafter I shall be united in all eternity to the one darling girl who has stuck to me through all this ordeal."

Whilst waiting for the death sentence to be carried out, Browne tried to commit suicide. Paradoxically, perhaps, enormous effort was put in to saving his life, so that he could survive long enough to be hung.

Browne and Kennedy were executed at 9 a.m. on 31 May 1928.

5 Murder by Moonlight

* * *

In the final phase of his career, Percy Savage became one of the so-called "Big Four" — the four senior detectives controlling the operational work of the C.I.D. in London.

In 1931, as part of the "Big Four", Percy Savage became involved in the Clay Lane murder case.

* * *

Edgware, North West London

May 1931

* * *

In the 1930s, the area round Clay Lane in Edgware still had a surprisingly rural feel: despite the encroachment of development, it was still possible to get a sense that this outer corner of London had once been a place of undulating woods and meadows.

Dense, secluded woodland surrounded Clay Lane, and it was this which attracted a community of itinerant workers to find shelter here. Clay Lane was, probably, London's last shanty town, an informal settlement of roughly built shacks.

The men of Clay Lane (and it appears to have been just men, rather than families) had a simple life-style. Most looked for any work which could be done with a pick and shovel. During the day, they would build sewers, reservoirs or roads; at night they would return to their crude Clay Lane shelters, built out of timber, tarpaulins and scavenged floor boards.

William Shelly, aged 57, and Oliver Newman, aged 61, were two of the men living in the Clay Lane shanty town. Shelley was known by his nickname, 'Moosh' or 'Essex Moosh'; Newman was known as 'Tiggy'. Moosh and Tiggy shared a hut in a clearing in the woods. Into their hut they had introduced some comforts: the ground was covered with timber, and they had two straw mattresses, some bedding and a cooking brazier. Illumination was provided by candles.

In mid-1931, Moosh and Tiggy were engaged on a road building project. After a day's work, they would buy some food and walk back to Clay Lane, often stopping on the way for a drink or two at a roadside pub. After supper, they would then sleep until the early hours, before cooking breakfast on the brazier, and heading off for a day's digging.

Moosh and Tiggy's hut was about a mile west of the Scratchwood rail sidings, running off the main railway line. The London, Midland, and Scottish Railway Company (LMSR) used Scratchwood as a vast dump, bringing in rubbish from all parts of their system, and burning it. The fire at Scratchwood never went out (it was said to have been alight continuously since the building of the railway line, some 70 years earlier). People in the local area were aware of the existence of the dump because of the large plume of smoke rising from it at all times of day and night.

At 5 p.m. on 1 June 1931, another Clay Lane dweller, a labourer called Michael McGlade, was preparing tea outside his shack. McGlade lived close to the Scratchwood dump and, finding that he had run out of matches, walked to the dump in order to get a light from the ever-smouldering fire.

As McGlade walked up to the dump, he was shocked to see a human hand sticking out from a bank of rubbish. Approaching closer, he could see the shape of a human body, covered by rags and gently burning waste. McGlade hurried to the Watford bypass, where he flagged down two policemen travelling on a motorcycle and side-car. The officers were on their way back from investigating some burglaries at the Moat Mount Golf Course. Dismounting, the officers followed McGlade on foot back to the dump.

When the officers saw that McGlade was telling the truth about the discovery of a body, one of them went back to the bypass to get more help, whilst the other stayed with McGlade. At some risk to himself, this officer clambered up the bank of rubbish and pulled the body out of the embers. The body was that of a powerfully built man. Burnt sacking was wrapped around his head, and part of the face had burnt away; the right forearm and both feet had also burnt away.

The C.I.D. responded quickly to the news that a body had been found. Percy Savage, as area Superintendent, took charge of the investigation: in his team were Divisional Detective Inspector Bennett from 'S' Division (covering an area running from north-west London to Hertfordshire) and Inspector Andrews. Savage, Bennett and Andrews arrived at the dump by car as soon as they could. Sir Bernard Spilsbury, the pathologist with whom Savage had worked on so many occasions, was also called.

Savage's first thought was that the body had arrived at Scratchwood by rail. The LMSR operated over a large territory, through the Midlands and the north west of England, as well as parts of Wales and Scotland. Savage made it a priority to cooperate with the railway police, in order to identify LMSR stations from which rubbish had been taken over the preceding few days. Police also made enquiries about ways in which the body might have reached the dump by road.

At the same time, Sergeant Prickett, a uniformed officer, started making enquiries locally. Sergeant Prickett was very familiar with the area, and knew about the huts and shacks around Clay Lane. He spoke to an itinerant navvy called James King, who told Prickett that another navvy, who he knew as 'Pigsticker', had not been seen for two or three days.

By now, the body found on the dump had been taken to the mortuary, and King was asked if he could identify it. Although the condition of the body made identification difficult, King thought that he could recognise the remnants of Pigsticker's moustache on the charred face. He was also able to confirm that bits of clothing worn by the dead man belonged to Pigsticker.

After enquiries, it was established that Pigsticker was Herbert William Ayres, a 45 year old Wiltshire-born man, whose family had moved up to Hertfordshire when he was fairly young. Ayres was one of seven children, and police managed to find his younger brother, Edward Ayres, a labourer, who was living in Watford. Edward was shown the body, and he confirmed that the body was that of his brother, partly because of a distinctive tattoo on the torso.

It was now Sir Bernard Spilsbury's job to give an opinion as to the cause of death. Although Ayres' face was charred, enough remained of his head for Spilsbury to identify holes in the skull, caused by blows from a heavy implement, such as an axe. It appeared that Ayres had been murdered before being moved to the dump, in the hope that fire would dispose of the body.

Police now had a name for the victim and a cause of death. The next task was to find out who killed him.

The answer to this question came from another navvy who lived in the shanty town. John Armstrong — known as 'Jordie' — had worked in different parts of the country, although he had strong connections with this area of north west London. He had been away from London for a long time, but had returned a few days before, and had arranged to share Moosh and Tiggy's hut.

According to Armstrong, on the night of Saturday 30 May, he had been drinking with Pigsticker in a pub in Edgware. At about 9 p.m., Armstrong left the pub and walked back to Moosh and Tiggy's hut, and went to sleep on a mattress. Although there were no candles alight in the hut, it was a night of an almost full moon, and the sky was clear: Armstrong remembered the moon shining brightly.

At about 10.50 p.m., he was woken by the arrival of Moosh and Tiggy.

"Are you there?" asked Moosh.

"Yes," Armstrong replied. Moosh and Tiggy walked away. Armstrong described what happened next:

> "Half an hour later, I heard several thuds, and a man cried, 'Oh, dear'. I sat up and then in the light of the moon I saw Moosh and Tiggy striking Pigsticker on the head. One of them used what looked like a blunderbuss. A few minutes later — it was about midnight — I heard more thuds, and then Moosh and Tiggy came and dropped an axe in a pail of water. Then I saw Moosh and Tiggy carrying a body in a sack through which they had thrust a pole. They went in the direction of Scratchwood sidings, and an hour or so later they returned to the hut. I was afraid to say anything and took no notice of them, because I knew what a violent temper they had. They lay down and went to sleep, and at four o'clock they got up and lit a fire, and Moosh washed his hat."

Armstrong was clearly frightened of Moosh and Tiggy. Having stayed quietly on his mattress throughout the murder, he packed his belongings and left the next morning. He was aware that being a witness to murder whilst still living with the murderers would have put him in a vulnerable position.

As he was leaving, Moosh came up and said "Jordie, if anybody says anything to you about Pigsticker . . . " Armstrong replied "I know all about it. Mum's the word."

Further evidence came from two other shanty town dwellers. Fred Cousins had been with Pigsticker on the evening of 30 May. Cousins and Pigsticker were sitting on a bus at Edgware Station, when Tiggy and Moosh looked inside the bus, and nodded towards Pigsticker. Then Tiggy undid his coat, and Cousins saw something which looked like an axe tucked into Tiggy's belt.

Later that night, Richard Saunders, who lived in an old van in Clay Lane, saw Tiggy and Moosh in 'The Boot', a pub in the Edgware Road. Saunders thought that Tiggy and Moosh were looking 'savage'. Tiggy told him "There will be something up if anyone comes 'mooshing' round our place." Saunders thought that Tiggy and Moosh might be threatening him, but they told him that Pigsticker was the man they had in mind.

* * *

Sergeant Prickett knew Moosh and Tiggy, although he was unaware that their real names were Shelly and Newman. Moosh and Tiggy's hut was in a fairly isolated spot, and police knew that it would be difficult to approach the hut without being heard. Given Shelley and Newman's alleged violence, police would have to go in force, and with some stealth, in order to effect an arrest.

After dark, a number of officers left their cars near the Watford bypass and, guided by Sergeant Prickett, moved up Clay Lane on foot. Strict silence was maintained, and the officers spread out to minimise the noise of their walking. When they got close to the clearing, they had to move through thick undergrowth, until stopping just short of the hut. They then stayed in position until dawn.

At 7 a.m., Moosh left the hut and walked through the woods. As he walked, Inspector Bennett jumped out of his hiding-place and arrested him. It appears that Tiggy, still in the hut, was unaware of what had happened. At about 7.30 a.m., Tiggy came out of the hut, and was captured. Then, Detective Superintendent Savage and Inspector Bennett searched the hut, finding a blood-stained axe under the floor boards.

At the police station, Moosh and Tiggy gave statements. What emerged was that the murder had been carried out as a reprisal.

Pigsticker had been stealing from Moosh and Tiggy's hut. In the unwritten law of the shanty town, stealing from another hut-dweller was regarded as a serious offence.

Moosh's statement read:

"I have been employed as a navvy in all parts of England and on the Continent. I came to Edgware about seven years ago and built myself a hut in Clay Lane. Tiggy came to live with me.

Last April Pigsticker put up a hut near to mine. He has been causing trouble all the time he has been in the lane. Two or three times last week I lost some tea and sugar, and Tiggy and I caught him stealing it. I went out after him, but he ran away.

I talked it over and decided to knock him about for it. About midday on Saturday, May 30th, when Tiggy and I got to our hut, we missed half a loaf of bread and some bacon, and we knew he had it. We did not see him, but we tracked his footprints. About 11.30 the same night, Pigsticker was outside my hut, and we accused him of stealing things, and then we both went outside to him. Pigsticker punched me in the chest and knocked me down. Then the fight started, and Tiggy joined in.

We had a terrible fight, and Pigsticker was killed. After that Tiggy and I took him up, and as he was bleeding very much from the face, we wrapped a piece of sacking round his head. We then carried him across to the shoot at Scratchwood sidings, a mile away, and laid him on some rubbish on the bank.

We then came home and went to bed. If I could have had my way, you would not have had us. I wanted to put him on the line and let a train hit him, but Tiggy would not have it. But still, he only got what he has been asking for, for a long time. The hardest job I have ever done was to carry him across there. We put him in a sack and put a pole through it."

Tiggy's statement gave a similar account:

> "We had some words with Pigsticker for pinching our stuff. Then we had a go for two minutes. I saw Pigsticker on the ground. I said to Moosh: 'He must be dead'. Then we carried him away over to the dust shoot, and we put him on the top and let him roll down."

* * *

The trial of Shelly and Newman opened at the Old Bailey on 24 June, 1931 — less than a month after the murder had been committed. The trial was very short, lasting only two days. According to Percy Savage, "during the two days the trial lasted, their real names — Shelley and Newman — were rarely heard. To the judge, counsel, jury and witnesses they were known as Moosh and Tiggy, and so accustomed was the court to hearing these names that it is possible nobody would have been surprised if the judge had used them when he sentenced the men to death".

Observers at the trial felt that Moosh and Tiggy did not really understand the gravity of the proceedings. It was as if they had stepped out of one world — the world of Clay Lane — into the mainstream world where, unbeknown to them, different rules applied.

The pair managed to find some humour in the trial. When 'Jordie' Armstrong was questioned about how he could be so certain about the time that the murder was committed, he produced a small alarm clock which he said had been in Moosh and Tiggy's hut. On hearing this, Moosh turned to Tiggy and said: "Gor' blimy Tiggy, he's pinched our clock."

Then, when the pair were sentenced to death, Moosh said to the judge "Thank you sir, it ought to have been years ago".

After sentence had been passed, Moosh asked Tiggy "How much money have you got?"

"Only twenty-five bob," Tiggy replied.

"I've only got eleven bob," said Moosh "and we ain't got much time to spend it."

Moosh and Tiggy were hung on 5 August, 1931.

* * *

The Scratchwood dump is now the site of the motorway service station known as London Gateway Services. Although Clay Lane still exists, much of the surrounding area has become built up.

THE UNSOLVED MURDER FILE

* * *

Not all murder cases are solved. Often, it is unsolved cases which continue to be intriguing: many years after the original crime, people carry on coming forward with theories about the identity of the murderer.

The final section of 'A Scotland Yard Murder Casebook' brings together two cases which remain mysteries. Both cases occurred early in Percy Savage's career, when he was a Detective Sergeant.

* * *

6 The Camberley Mystery

* * *

Heathfield House, London Road, Camberley, Surrey.

11 June 1906

* * *

The Hogg sisters lived a quiet life. Mary Anne Hogg, 69, and Caroline Gwinnell Hogg, 62, were "ladies of independent means". Having inherited a large amount of money, they lived in Heathfield House, on the outskirts of Camberley.

Set back from the Camberley-Bagshot road, Heathfield was a substantial red brick house with a commanding frontage, approached by a carriage drive. The sisters kept a horse-drawn carriage and, when the weather was fine, would amuse themselves by riding out into the surrounding countryside.

At home, they enjoyed the substantial gardens surrounding Heathfield; on fine days, Mary Anne insisted that the front door was kept open so that fresh air could flow through the house.

This peaceful existence came to an end on the afternoon of Monday, 11 June 1906.

Shortly after 4 p.m., Caroline Hogg ran into the grounds of Heathfield, shouting for help. Her throat had been cut, and she was bleeding profusely from a number of head wounds.

A local postman heard Caroline's shouts, and ran up the drive to the house, only to find another more gruesome sight. The body of Mary Anne Hogg was lying in the hall, face down in a pool of blood. Her throat had been cut, leaving a wound which ran from ear to ear: the wound was so deep that her head was partly severed from her body. She had a number of other head wounds.

Alerted by the postman, two police officers from the local force — Constables Holdaway and Brown — arrived at the house shortly afterwards, followed by two doctors. One of the doctors noted that Mary Anne Hogg's body was still warm. Examination of the body also revealed a piece of evidence. Mary Anne was grasping the head of a hammer in one of her hands. The hammer head was wrapped in cloth. As her body was moved, her hand opened and the hammer head clattered to the floor. The handle of the hammer was lying a short distance away.

There appeared to be little other evidence to explain what had happened. Caroline Hogg was too distressed to give a coherent witness statement, although she was able to say that she had been attacked by a man with what she thought was a tall axe, like a pole-axe. There was an area of woodland behind the house. An intruder could easily have approached the house, and escaped, without being noticed. However, there was no sign of forced entry, and no obvious footprints.

The pattern of blood stains in the house did not give much further help. There was blood at the front door, and a trail of blood leading through the hall to the back door. There were also spots of blood in the basement, suggesting that, unless the attacker had been wounded, one of the sisters had gone down there. A bowl of water with some blood in it was also found: this had been used by somebody to wash their bloodstained hands, or to wash blood off an object, such as a murder weapon. However, no knife or sharp implement appeared to be lying around.

* * *

Faced with this brutal double attack, Surrey police decided that it was necessary to call in Scotland Yard. In doing so, a small milestone in the history of British policing was passed. Only a couple of months earlier, the Home Office had formalized a scheme where police forces outside London could call on the detective expertise of the Metropolitan Police. The Camberley mystery was the first case in which a local force had "called in Scotland Yard" using this scheme.

Within 24 hours, Detective Chief Inspector Fox, Detective Sergeant Brown and Detective Sergeant Percy Savage arrived from London.

At this stage in his career, Percy Savage was serving in the Metropolitan Police's 'M' Division in Southwark. Southwark had a reputation as a 'tough' area: Savage commented that he was "surprised at the number of criminals found within a stone's throw of Borough High Street". Given Southwark's reputation, it is ironic, perhaps, that one of the most vicious assaults which Savage dealt with whilst in 'M' Division occurred 30 miles out of London, in leafy Surrey.

* * *

Heathfield House, its grounds, and the woods behind were searched. Ditches and hedges were scoured. The hammer, the head of which had been grasped in Mary Anne Hogg's hand, was found to be a bricklayer's hammer, taken from a shed in the garden.

Still no trace could be found of the implement which had been used to cut the sisters' throats. Despite thorough examination, no unusual finger-prints could be found. The last person known to have visited the house was a baker's boy who delivered a loaf of bread to the house at 3 p.m.. He saw nothing suspicious.

Professor Pepper, the Home Office pathologist, was called to the scene. He found that Mary Anne Hogg's head had five hammer marks on it, but it was not fractured. Her head wounds were similar to those suffered by Caroline Hogg, so Pepper concluded that they were caused by the same hammer. Pepper's theory was that each woman was attacked on the head first: once this had stunned them or made them unconscious, their throats were cut. Mary Ann Hogg's throat wound was so deep that it must have been made with great force. Pepper also concluded that the wounds were "homicidal not suicidal" — in other words, the wounds were not self-inflicted.

The case quickly attracted the attention of the press, with journalists labelling it "The Camberley Outrage" or "The Pole-axe Murder". At first, it was widely assumed that the motive for the attack had been robbery. A newspaper report on the day after the attack said "that the two ladies were in the habit of keeping in the house large sums of money, and there is little doubt locally that the murderer had become acquainted with this fact, and that robbery was the motive for the crime."

Other newspaper stories referred to suspicious sightings, but it is unclear to what extent these reports were based on anything more substantial than rumour. One newspaper described a statement made by a bank manager from Camberley:

> "He states that when walking with his wife along London Road on Monday afternoon he noticed a man in a stooping position immediately outside the hedge which borders the drive of Heathfield. His attention was drawn to this person, by the fact that after regaining his ordinary posture he hesitated a moment, as if undecided which direction to take, and then walked briskly towards Bagshot. The man, who carried a large paper bag, was dressed in the clothes of a respectable merchant."

Caroline Hogg offered a £200 reward (about £23,000 in today's money) for information leading to the arrest of the murderer. The team from Scotland Yard, acting in cooperation with local officers, interviewed people living nearby, whilst reviewing the records of criminals whose previous offences suggested that they were capable of an attack of this sort.

However, when nobody could find the mystery man who was supposed to have attacked the sisters, attention turned to the sisters themselves. In the absence of solid information, speculation and gossip filled the void. Percy Savage summarised some of the ideas whirling around:

> "It might be thought, for example, that some romantic incident in the lives of the two sisters had led them to enter a suicide pact, or that they had quarrelled, and had fought each other until death put an end to the combat."

Conscious that she was now under suspicion, Caroline Hogg was at pains to emphasise that she and Mary Anne had been on friendly terms. The two women were, in fact, half sisters whose inherited money came from their father. After the attack, Caroline claimed that she had more money than her sister, presumably to dispel any idea that she would benefit financially from her sister's death.

Caroline also explained how dependent she had been on Mary Anne. Caroline was described in press reports as an invalid and appears to have left the day-to-day running of the house to her elder sister. According to Caroline, Mary Anne "did everything for her", which included doing the cooking and waiting on her at times when there were no servants in the house.

* * *

There was absolutely no evidence to show that Caroline Hogg had been involved in the attack, other than as a victim. Despite this, by the time that the inquest into Mary Anne's death opened, some people felt that Caroline Hogg had failed to give a full enough account of the attack. Jurors at the inquest, held at the newly built Camberley Police Court, were allowed to put questions to witnesses: some jurors asked Caroline questions which verged on the hostile.

As part of the Scotland Yard team, Percy Savage noted his frustration with the fact that Caroline Hogg's evidence "was very vague and puzzling, but that was not altogether surprising considering the ordeal she had gone through. However, we had to be content with her hazy recollection of events. She could not even tell us which way the assailant had made his escape."

At the coroner's court, Caroline Hogg wore a black veil, and her head was wrapped in black bandages. She was accompanied by a nurse, who helped her to move around the court room. The following account of Caroline Hogg's evidence, and her questioning by the coroner, give a good idea of the uncertainty which still surrounded the murder.

"My sister and I," said Caroline Hogg "occupied separate bedrooms, and we also had our own dressing-room. My room was in the western part of the house, and my sister occupied the central position."

"On the day of the murder," asked the coroner, "what time did you get up?"

"Between two and three o'clock in the afternoon."

"Did you see your sister in the morning or in the early afternoon?"

"She came into my bedroom between two and three. That was before I got up."

"May I take it that it was not your habit to get up until the afternoon?"

"Well, not until after twelve o'clock."

"Did you have breakfast or lunch that day?"

"No, nothing at all."

"What took place when your sister came into the room?"

"She said she had put the carriage off. We had arranged to go for a drive. I think she said it would not be fine enough to go for a drive, and she had a headache."

"Then there were several reasons — headache, likely to be rain, and so on. Did she tell you all that?"

"I said: 'I am sorry you put the carriage off'."

"Did she say anything to you about getting up?"

"No. She went downstairs."

"How soon afterwards did you get up?"

"It was between three and four."

"Did you hear anything?"

"I heard what I thought was a slight exclamation. At first I thought it was my sister calling me, but in thinking of it afterwards I think it was an exclamation."

"What did you do?"

"I got to the head of the stairs along the passage, when I met a man. He said: 'I want money.' I told him the money was downstairs."

"What sort of a man was he?"

"He was dressed as a bricklayer with his sleeves tucked up. His face was red and he had dark eyes, and he had a light-coloured string net over his face."

"Was the net tied round his throat, or was it loose?"

"It was hanging loose. When I told him the money was downstairs he made no further remark but ran downstairs. We both rushed downstairs together but I could not say who went first. I have an idea that I went first and he followed close after me. I then saw my sister in the garden in front of the house facing the front door with blood streaming down her face. I was going through the front door when the man struck me and I fell. I then, for the first time, saw something like a pickaxe or a hammer in his hand. It had a long handle, and the man held it in both hands. I thought he must have picked it up in the hall, as I noticed nothing in his hands on the stairs. My sister came in from the garden, and I heard her exclaim: 'Oh!'."

"When your sister came in from the garden, do you suggest that she was stunned?"

"No, I think she was dazed. My hair, I think I ought to tell you, was twisted round my head just where the blows came, and I think that saved my head a little. I struggled to the door. I do not recollect when my throat was cut, but I think it was done at the door."

"During this time did you speak to your sister?"

"No, it all happened almost simultaneously. It was all done in about half a minute."

"What, from the time you first saw him on the stairs until you got out?"

"Yes."

"And in that half minute, although the man had a net on, you were able to notice that he had a red face and dark eyes?"

"Yes."

"When you got up and struggled to the door, did you see your sister?"

"Yes, she was standing by me. We were both near the dock, and the man was trying to prevent us from getting out of the door. The man followed me into the garden."

"And your sister was in the garden?"

"Yes, we all three went into the garden. We went as far as the doorstep, and I rushed to the gate to get assistance. The only things missing from the house were a purse and a George the Third prayer book."

* * *

The coroner's jury returned a verdict of wilful murder by person or persons unknown . After the inquest, the police investigation continued, and the three man team from Scotland Yard remained in Surrey for a total of six weeks. After the inquest, the police received a report of a man seen scrambling through a hedge in the garden of Heathfield House, but this man was never identified.

Percy Savage acknowledged that: "All was in vain, and we returned to London without the satisfaction of being able to clear up the mystery." Nevertheless, Savage thought that the Camberley case had been a useful experience. The murder came at a time when detective methods were developing and becoming more methodical, and Savage felt that the investigation was well conducted:

" . . . although in spite of all our efforts we were unable to bring the murderer to justice, the case afforded a valuable illustration of the advantage of employing experienced detectives in the investigation of all crimes . . . The case aroused a keener interest in crime investigation. County and local police forces realized their responsibilities to a greater degree than they ever did before . . . "

Over a hundred years later, the Camberley mystery remains unsolved.

7 The Luard Case

* * *

Seal Chart, Kent
August 1908

* * *

Major-General Charles Luard was the model of an Edwardian country gentleman. After a distinguished career in the Army, he retired to the country, living at Ightham Knoll in a beautiful part of the Kent Weald. His house was full of military and sporting trophies. When in London, the Major-General would visit his club, the Naval and Military in Piccadilly; back in the country, he would pursue his hobbies, which he listed in *Who's Who* as "fishing, golf and shooting".

He was married to Caroline, the daughter of a wealthy banking family. By all accounts, Charles and Caroline Luard were devoted to each other. The area around their house was criss-crossed with paths and bridleways, and they were frequently seen roaming arm-in-arm through the country lanes, "looking like a honeymoon couple" as one neighbour put it.

It was on one of their walks that tragedy struck.

On Friday 24 August 1908, Charles and Caroline Luard left Ightham Knoll at about 2.30 p.m., accompanied by their terrier. Their walk took them through Fish Pond Woods, part of the nearby Frankfield estate. This was owned by the Wilkinson family, with whom the Luard's were friendly. On the edge of Fish Pond Woods, close to a place known as Crown Point, there was a small summer house, known as the 'Casa'. The 'Casa' was a peaceful spot, with views over the 'Casa pond' and woodland beyond. The Luards and the Wilkinsons often took tea together at the 'Casa'.

After walking for about half an hour, the Major-General and his wife reached a small gate on the path near St Lawrence's Church. At this point, the couple went separate ways. Charles Luard, accompanied by the terrier, continued in the direction of the Wildernesse golf course at Godden Green. His aim was to collect his golf-clubs in preparation for a forthcoming holiday.

At the same time, Caroline turned round and re-traced her steps through Fish Pond Woods. Caroline was heading back to Ightham Knoll, where a friend of hers, Mary Stewart, would shortly be arriving for tea.

By about 3.30 p.m., Charles Luard had collected his golf clubs from Godden Green, and had started to walk home. On his walk back he was spotted by the Reverend Arthur Cotton, the Vicar of Shipbourne, a nearby village. Cotton was driving in the opposite direction, but stopped to offer Luard a lift. Luard thanked him and said that he would prefer to continue his journey on foot. Cotton drove off, but a little while later he found himself passing Luard again — this time on the main Sevenoaks-Ightham road. Cotton repeated his offer of a lift, and Luard accepted: the Major-General "looked hot and tired" according to Cotton. Cotton dropped Luard off at Ightham Knoll close to 4.30 p.m..

Mrs. Stewart, Caroline Luard's tea guest, was already at Ightham Knoll; Caroline, however, had not arrived. Charles Luard apologised for his wife's absence, but reassured Mrs. Stewart that she was bound to be back home in a few minutes.

After waiting for five minutes, Charles Luard and Mrs. Stewart decided to have tea, before going in search of Caroline Luard. Leaving Ightham Knoll, they walked towards Fish Pond Woods. However, at a point known as Seven Wents, Mrs. Stewart decided to go back, because she had arranged to meet a friend at home at 5.15 p.m..

Charles Luard carried on alone, retracing the route which he and his wife had walked earlier that afternoon. Approaching the 'Casa', the Major-General was shocked to see his wife lying face-down on the wooden veranda at the front of the summer house. His first thought was that she had fainted but, as he ran towards her, he saw that she was lying in a pool blood. Caroline Luard was dead.

Although an old soldier, nothing had prepared Charles Luard for a scene like this, and for a moment he felt helpless. However, he knew that he must get help, so he walked to the stables on the Wilkinson's estate, about three quarters of a mile (1,200 metres) away. Here, at 5.55 p.m., he found the Wilkinson's butler, Herbert Harding.

"My wife is dead," Luard shouted "Do come with me."

Harding wondered if the Major-General had made a mistake, and asked "Has she fainted?"

"No" Luard replied "It's worse than that."

Luard and Harding hurried to the 'Casa'. Police and doctors were also telephoned. At about 7.40 p.m., Dr. Mansfield arrived from Sevenoaks.

In the failing light, Dr. Mansfield made careful notes. Caroline Luard's hands were raised above her head, which was about a foot from the steps leading up to the verandah. She had vomited. Her right cheek was facing downwards. There were two bullet holes in her head, each of about the same size: one was behind her right ear, and the other on her left temple.

She also had a wound, not caused by a shot, at the back of her head. Her right cheek, chin and nose were bruised. The straw hat which she had worn that afternoon was lying about an arm's length away from her head. The hat, trimmed in black ribbon, was blood-stained, and had a dent at the back, in a position which corresponded to the wound at the back of her head.

Her right hand was still gloved, but her left-hand glove had been taken off, turned inside out, and dropped near her body, as if the glove had been pulled off in a hurry. There were also small abrasions on two of the fingers on her left hand, where three of her rings had been pulled off. These rings were missing.

Her dress was torn: a pocket on the back of the dress had been ripped open, and the purse which she kept in it had disappeared.

Dr. Mansfield reached the conclusion that Caroline Luard had been struck on the back of the head by a heavy stick or a similar heavy object, before being shot twice at close range by a small-calibre revolver. He also judged that the shot behind her ear was fired first; this had failed to kill her, leading to a second shot being fired at the left side of her face.

The other medical practitioner who arrived at the 'Casa', Dr. Walker, took a different view of one detail. He argued that the wound at the back of Caroline Luard's head had been caused by her falling against a stone pillar at the front of the veranda. Both men, however, agreed that this was not a case of suicide. No revolver or cartridges could be found at the scene: it was, in any case, hard to see how Caroline Luard could have shot herself twice.

With suicide ruled out, a murder hunt started. The Chief Constable of Kent, Lieutenant Colonel Henry Warde was a good friend of Major-General Luard. Warde asked Luard to write a full statement, describing his movements, and those of his wife on the afternoon of the murder.

Luard's statement set out the route of the walk through Fish Pond Woods, his own walk to the golf course, his return to Ightham Knoll with his golf clubs, and the discovery of his wife's body. In his statement, Luard was also able to clarify other details — for example, that his wife wore all her rings on the left hand, and always wore them, except when she washed her hands.

* * *

Realising the importance of the case, Lieutenant Colonel Warde devoted considerable resources to it, allocating Superintendents Taylor and Ford, as well as Detective Inspector Fowle from Maidstone, to the investigation. On 26 August, the day that the inquest into the murder opened, the Chief Constable also decided that, in the absence of any obvious leads, it was necessary to call in Scotland Yard.

By now, Percy Savage had been promoted to first-class sergeant and transferred to 'A' Division — the Division which operates out of Scotland Yard itself. Savage became the junior member of the Scotland Yard team assigned to the Luard case, working under Chief-Inspector Scott. According to Savage: "From the first it was evident that the task of finding the murderer would be extremely difficult, if not absolutely impossible, and this fact only made us the keener".

The obvious starting point for the investigation was the Major-General's statement. Charles Luard was the last person known to have seen his wife alive; he was also the first person to have found her dead at the 'Casa'.

Scott and Savage reviewed Luard's statement. Savage quickly reached the conclusion that "his written statement was as full and as clear as one could expect considering the mental stress under which he was suffering." However, all of the points in the statement had to be checked before it could be decided whether the Major-General was innocent.

Witness statements suggested that Caroline Luard had been murdered at 3.15 p.m.. Annie Wickham, the 58 year old wife of Mr. Wilkinson's coachman, lived in a lodge on the Wilkinson's estate. At 3.15 p.m. she had been about 550 yards (500 metres) from the summer house. She reported hearing a "very strange sound, as if something had been struck at close quarters", followed by two other sounds which she thought were like shots. However, this did not alarm her, as the use of sporting guns in Fish Pond Woods was a common occurrence.

Also at 3.15 p.m., Daniel Kettle, a 52 year old gardener working for the Wilkinsons, heard what he thought were three shots. Kettle was about a quarter of a mile (400 metres) from the 'Casa', and he reported that the sounds came from the direction of the summer house. Like Annie Wickham, he was not alarmed by the sound of shots, being used to people shooting in the woods.

If Caroline Luard was shot at 3.15 p.m., this made it necessary to be sure that the Major-General was nowhere near the summer house at the time. A number of people reported seeing Charles Luard after he and his wife went their separate ways near St. Lawrence's Church. At 3.20 p.m., a man called Thomas Durrant, a brewer's manager, saw Luard near Hall Farm, walking in the direction of the golf club. Durrant reported that Luard smiled at him and looked happy.

Between 3.25 and 3.30 p.m., Luard was seen by Ernest King, a labourer, some 400 yards from the golf course. At 3.35 p.m., Harry Kent, the steward at Godden Green Club House saw Luard on the golf course itself. Between 3.35 and 3.40pm, Ernest King saw Luard again, carrying golf clubs on his return journey.

To test these timings, Superintendent Taylor from Kent Police walked from Ightham Knoll to the golf club, using the route which Luard said he had taken. At a normal pace, the whole journey took one hour and one minute, and the section between the summer house and the golf club took half an hour. This strongly suggested that Luard was nowhere near the summer house at 3.15 p.m.. If he had been at the summer house at that time, he would have had to have run at some speed in order to get to the golf course by 3.30 p.m.. Luard, although fit, was 69 years of age; in addition, when he was seen at 3.20 p.m. and then between 3.25 p.m. and 3.30 p.m., he was walking, not running.

One other possibility had to be considered — what if the murder had not taken place at 3.15 p.m.? As we have seen, at that time, Annie Wickham and Daniel Kettle heard sounds which they took to be shots. However, what if these sounds were not actually the shots which killed Caroline Luard? The police knew that, on that day, there were a number of people out shooting in the area.

The police conducted experiments which showed that the sound of an ordinary revolver fired at the summer house could be heard clearly about a fifth of a mile (or a third of a kilometre) away. This made it seem likely that the sounds heard by the two witnesses at 3.15 p.m. were those of the shots fired at the 'Casa', although there was still scope for doubt.

Another question to consider was motive. The police could not find any reason why Major-General Luard would want to murder his wife. Percy Savage commented that:

"It is often an unpleasant business, this task of endeavouring to find hidden motives. It involves delving into past years and bringing back to persons memories of things they had long forgotten and would probably prefer to remain forgotten. So far as the General was concerned, we could find not the slightest reason why he should have committed the crime. He was in perfectly sound health, both bodily and mentally, so there was no question of a sudden homicidal impulse."

According to Savage, the police found that Charles Luard lived happily with his wife:

" . . . the servants in the house described them as a devoted couple. They were never heard to quarrel, and on the day of the tragedy they appeared to be as happy as they always had been. He had no monetary worries, nor would he benefit monetarily by her death. Three rings had been torn off her left hand, and her dress pocket had been cut out and the purse extracted from it. If the husband had committed the murder, would he have been so utterly callous and so devoid of human feeling as to rob his dead wife in such a brutal manner?"

Another thing which had to be investigated was the fact that Luard kept three revolvers at his house — one in the kitchen, another in the bathroom, and the third in his study. These were, he explained, for protection against burglars. The police submitted these revolvers to Edwin Churchill, a firearms expert, who confirmed that they were a different calibre from the murder weapon, which was assessed to be a .320 revolver.

If Major-General Luard was not the murderer, who was? Two different theories emerged to explain Caroline Luard's death.

The first theory was that her death was the result of a bungled robbery. Perhaps a tramp, or a fruit or hop picker, had been nosing round the summer house, but was disturbed by Caroline Luard on her walk: events had then unfolded in an unplanned but dramatic way.

This theory gained some of its force from the fact that, in summer, Kent filled up with casual workers hired to pick strawberries, cherries, blackberries and vegetables. These workers often lived rough in temporary shelters put up in secluded areas like woodland. The hop picking season was also about to start: traditionally, this brought in whole families from London's East End.

Many Kent residents were suspicious of the temporary workers passing through their county and, fairly or unfairly, often blamed them for an increase in petty crime. An indication of the hostile reception given to the temporary pickers was that some pub landlords would only serve them beer in jam jars, supposedly to avoid the regular beer tankards being stolen.

Interestingly, Reverend Cotton — the Vicar who had given Charles Luard a lift —reported seeing an unknown man near Crown Point on the day of the murder. Cotton was taking a party of ladies in his car on what was described as "a photographic expedition" and, passing Crown Point just before 4 p.m., he saw a man emerge from Fish Pond Woods. Cotton said that the man was aged about 40, had 3 or 4 days growth of stubble, and a "low type of face". He added that he would recognise the man if he saw him again.

From a police point of view, the problem with the theory that a passing stranger killed Caroline Luard is that it seemed unlikely that a tramp, a casual fruit picker, or a hop picker would go about armed with a revolver, let alone use it to kill a woman for the sake of three rings and a purse. Police interviewed tramps who had been in the neighbourhood. They also questioned residents in Ightham, Seal, Ivy Hatch and Shipbourne, but could find nobody who had seen a stranger hanging around the countryside at the relevant time.

The second theory was that Caroline Luard's murder was a pre-meditated crime, carried out by (or on behalf of) somebody with a grudge against the Luards. Whilst Charles Luard was in the Army, he had become involved in a messy dispute about who was to blame for the defeat of British forces in an engagement during the Anglo-Zulu war. During the dispute, tempers flared and accusations and counter-accusations were flung about by members of the British officer corps.

However, this had all taken place nearly 30 years earlier. It seemed unlikely, after the passage of so many years, that somebody would return to pursue a grudge by killing the Major-General's wife. The other problem with the idea that this was a pre-meditated murder is that nobody could have known beforehand which route the Luards were going to follow on their walk. They often took different paths and byways and, according to Charles Luard, on the day of the murder did not make up their mind which way they were going until after leaving Ightham Knoll.

With no suspects to interview, the police hoped that the objects taken from the murder scene would turn up and lead them to the murderer. Pawnbrokers and jewellers were approached, in case somebody tried to sell Caroline Laurd's rings, but this produced no information. The police also hoped that the pocket which had been ripped from Caroline Luard's dress might be found. However, on the day of Caroline Luard's funeral, a maid at Ightham Knoll, Jane

Pugmore, was shaking out the sheet in which Caroline Luard's body had been carried back from the summer house, and the pocket fell out: as such, it offered no clue as to the identity of the murderer.

* * *

The inquest into Caroline Luard's death opened on 26 August in the dining hall of Ightham Knoll. On the first day of the inquest, Charles Luard, Inspector Taylor of Kent police and Edwin Churchill, the firearms expert, gave evidence. The inquest was then adjourned for a fortnight to allow investigation into the death to continue, before re-opening, but this time at the George & Dragon Inn, Ightham.

The inquest gave Charles Luard an opportunity to clarify his story in public. The coroner asked the Major-General whether there had been "any incident in the life of the deceased or yourself which in your opinion would cause any person to entertain any feelings of revenge or jealousy towards either of you?". Luard replied with a firm "No". He also denied that somebody had written to his wife in order to make an appointment to see her.

The coroner asked Luard about the events of the day itself:

"Are you in the habit of carrying a revolver?"

"No."

"Had you one on the day in question?"

"No."

"You heard no shots after you left your wife?"

"No."

* * *

The inquest left the case unsolved, and there was nothing said that helped to identify the killer. The lack of conclusive evidence left the field open for an ugly rash of local gossip. Had Caroline

Luard been shot by a secret lover? Had Charles Luard shot his wife after discovering that she had a secret lover? Did Charles Luard have a lover, and hence a motive for wanting his wife out of the way? Perhaps Charles Luard's regular trips to the golf course had been a cover for an affair?

The rumours spread despite evidence that the Luards had enjoyed a happy marriage: at the inquest, Jane Pugmore, their maid, confirmed that she had never heard the couple quarrelling. Newspaper reports did not help the situation: for example, the *Daily Chronicle* reported the suggestion that the murderer had removed Caroline Luard's rings in an attempt to hide the true motive for her killing.

What followed was an upsetting campaign of anonymous letter-writing directed at Charles Luard. He received scores of letters accusing him of his wife's death: a number of these letters carried local postmarks. According to Bertram Winnifrith, a local clergyman and a friend of Luard's, the letters contained "vile effusions".

Understandably, the Major-General was deeply upset by these letters. In September 1908, he decided that he would move out of Ightham Knoll. On 16 September, he went to stay at Barham Court, the home of his friend, Charles Warde MP (who was also the Chief Constable's brother). That evening Luard dined with Charles Warde and his wife, Helen. However, the next morning he did not appear for breakfast.

A housemaid at Barham Court reported that Luard had left the house after having a morning cup of tea. Luard walked across the surrounding parkland, crossed the Maidstone Road, and followed a footpath to the railway line. Here, he hid in bushes until the 9 a.m. Maidstone to Paddock Wood train approached. Rushing out of the bushes, Luard threw himself in front of the train.

That day, he was due to go to Southampton to meet his son, an Army officer, who had returned home from South Africa after hearing of his mother's death.

Whilst he was drinking his cup of tea at Barham Court, the Major-General had written the following letter:

"My dear Warde,

I am sorry to have to return your kindness and hospitality and long friendship in this way, but I am satisfied it is best to join her in the second life at once, as I can be of no further use to anyone in future in this world, of which I am tired, and in which I do not wish to live any longer. I thought that my strength was sufficient to bear up against the horrible imputations and terrible letters which I have received since that awful crime was committed which robbed me of my happiness. And so it was for long, and the goodness, kindness and sympathy of so many friends kept me going. But somehow, in the last day or two, something seems to have snapped. The strength has left me, and I care for nothing except to join her again. So good-bye, dear friend, to both of us.

Yours very affectionately,

C.E. Luard.

P.S. I shall be somewhere on the line of railway."

As the *Maidstone & Kentish Journal* commented: "two murders have been committed in Kent . . . Mrs. Luard was killed with a pistol; General Luard was killed with a pen".

The inquest into Charles Luard's death was told that his suicide was due to the malicious letters which he had received. The coroner was keen to emphasise that Luard was not responsible for his wife's murder: "The General" he said "had absolutely accounted for all his movements on the day of the murder, and showed that he could not have been present and committed that terrible act."

* * *

Kent police kept the case open. At the beginning of November 1908, the Chief Constable of Kent offered a £1,000 reward to anyone who, by 1 January 1909, gave information leading to the apprehension or conviction of the murderer. Further searches took place near the 'Casa', with ponds being dragged and a well close to the summer house being drained, in an attempt to find the revolver and the missing rings.

In the summer of 1909, Kent police arrested David Woodruff, a homeless vagrant, who had been sentenced to four month's hard labour for threatening somebody with a revolver. On the day that Woodruff was due to be released from Maidstone Prison for this offence, he was re-arrested. On the following Monday, he was taken to Sevenoaks police court. At the court, Inspector Taylor told magistrates that the Chief Constable had evidence that Woodruff was the murderer of Caroline Luard. However, Taylor said that he was not in a position to put this evidence before the magistrates. As a result, the magistrates had no choice but to release Woodruff.

In fact, Kent police had no evidence that Woodruff was the killer. It later turned out that Woodruff had been in prison on the day of the murder.

The Woodruff arrest added fuel to the fire for the conspiracy theorists who thought that the Luard case involved some kind of establishment cover up. The suggestion was made that the Chief Constable of Kent believed that his friend Major-General Luard was guilty of the murder, and wanted to frame Woodruff for the offence in order to protect Luard's reputation. However, given that Luard was dead, it seems more feasible to suggest that the police were simply keen to find somebody guilty, and that Woodruff's profile — a vagrant who had carried a revolver — led them to over-reach themselves, and to pursue a case for which they had no evidence.

There is a further twist to the tale. In 1910, a man called John Dickman was sentenced to death for murdering a passenger on a train in Morpeth, Northumberland. The case against Dickman rested on shaky evidence and, after he was sentenced to death, there was a vigorous campaign calling for his reprieve. The case got as far as the Home Secretary, Winston Churchill, who refused to pardon Dickman.

A number of people have sought to make a connection between Dickman's conviction and the Luard mystery.

Sir Sidney Orme Rowan-Hamilton, a distinguished lawyer, developed an interest in the Dickman case. According to Rowan-Hamilton, in 1908 Dickman was involved in what would now be called a "charity scam". The scam involved Dickman placing an advertisement in *The Times*, asking for financial help for a deserving person in need. Caroline Luard responded to this advertisement, sending Dickman a cheque. According to Rowan-Hamilton, Dickman changed the amount on the cheque, fraudulently increasing the amount which he was to be paid. When Caroline Luard discovered this, she contacted Dickman and arranged to meet him, although without telling her husband about the plan. Dickman turned up at the 'Casa', where he murdered Caroline Luard.

Rowan-Hamilton also believed that Dickman was wrongly convicted for the Morpeth murder in 1910 and that this conviction was the result of a conspiracy between senior figures in the legal establishment, who wanted revenge for the killing of Caroline Luard. According to Rowan-Hamilton, the rejection of Dickman's appeal against his conviction, and Winston Churchill's refusal to grant him a pardon, could only be understood in this context.

It seems fair to argue that Dickman's conviction for the Morpeth railway killing was unsafe. However, although Rowan-Hamilton was an able lawyer (he later became Chief Justice of

Bermuda), it is also fair to say that there is a lack of evidence to support the allegation that the police, the judiciary and Winston Churchill took part in a concerted conspiracy, based on the belief that John Dickman was Caroline Luard's killer.

The Luard case remains a mystery.

* * *

Detective Superintendent Percy Savage retired in 1934. He moved to Torquay, where he died in 1943.

* * *

Printed in Great Britain
by Amazon